LEGACY

THE OFFICIAL

BOSTON CELTICS

1992 - 1993 GREENBOOK

By Roland Lazenby
Photographs by Steve Lipofsky
Statistics and player bios by David Zuccaro

LONGSTREET PRESS
Atlanta, Georgia

Published by Longstreet Press, Inc.
A subsidiary of Cox Newspapers, Inc.
2140 Newmarket Parkway
Suite 118
Marietta, Georgia 30067

Printed in the United States of America

1st printing, 1992

ISBN 1-56352-056-7

This book was printed by Semline, Inc., Westwood, Massachusetts

Jacket design by Jill Dible
Book design by Karen Snidow Lazenby

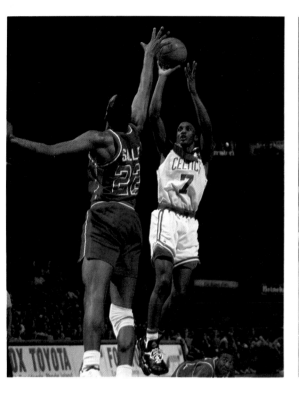

Contents

Larry and Magic made television a regular partner in the NBA.

Preface

Steve Lipofsky graces the pages with his stunning photography. His work has preserved the magic of the Bird era for seasons to come.

For historical perspective, we supplemented here and there with the work of long-time NBA photographer Ron Koch.

Once again, many thanks are in order for this edition of the *Greenbook*. First to Tod Rosensweig, the Celtics' vice president for communications, who edited and supervised the project. And to David Zuccaro, the Celtics' director of publications and information, who authored the player bios and compiled the statistics in the back matter. Plus Jeff Twiss, the Celtics' public relations director, was more than gracious in making sure materials and information were available.

The staff at Longstreet Press, particularly Walt Fuller, did much of the yeoman's work in pushing the *Greenbook* along. And my wife, Karen Snidow Lazenby, spent long hours seeing the book through the stages of electronic publishing.

Beyond that, the New England newspapers again supplied their excellent coverage of the team. The list of the best should include Peter May, Jackie MacMullan and Bob Ryan at the *Globe*. They were excellent, as were Steve Bulpett and Mark Murphy at the *Herald*, and Jim Fenton at the *Brockton Enterprise* and Mike Fine of the *Quincy Patriot Ledger*. Once again, their writing and reporting have made Bostonians the best-informed basketball fans in America.

The list of those granting interviews begins with Celtics' president Red Auerbach, who took the time to discuss events as he saw them. Others who graciously agreed to be interviewed were Chris Ford, Jan Volk, Bob Cousy, K.C. Jones, Magic Johnson, Gerald Henderson, Jerry Sichting, Ed Pinckney, Larry Bird, Robert Parish, Kevin McHale, Joe Kleine, Reggie Lewis, Don Casey, Jon Jennings, Kevin Gamble, Dee Brown and Rick Fox.

Extensive use was made of a variety of publications, including *The New York Times, Sports Illustrated, The Sporting News, Street & Smith's Pro Basketball Yearbook, USA Today* and *The Washington Post*.

The reporting work of a variety of writers helped tremendously: Jack Madden, Ted Green, Pat Putnam, Sandy Padwe, Jack McCallum, Sam Goldaper, Peter Vecsey, Alex Wolff and Bruce Newman.

Also, several books were key in my research, including: *Basketball for the Player, the Fan and the Coach,* by Red Auerbach; *College Basketball's 25 Greatest Teams,* by Billy Packer and Roland Lazenby; *Cousy on the Celtic Mystique* by Bob Cousy and Bob Ryan; *The Boston Celtics,* by Bob Ryan; *The Modern Basketball Encyclopedia,* by Zander Hollander; *The Official NBA Basketball Encyclopedia,* edited by Zander Hollander and Alex Sachare; and *Rick Barry's Pro Basketball Scouting Report,* by Rick Barry and Jordan E. Cohn.

Roland Lazenby

Bird was the heart of Boston's resurgence in the 1980s.

"The Hick from French Lick"

Camelot

I t's officially over now. Pro basketball's age of Camelot has ended. In retrospect, it was one of those rare situations where the legend couldn't outlast the reality.

The legend, of course, was Larry Joe Bird. And the reality was his aching, 35-year-old back, which finally forced him to announce his retirement August 18, 1992, ending speculation on whether he would attempt to return to the Boston Celtics for a fourteenth season.

"If I was healthy this year and I knew I could have helped my team, I would've played," Bird told a hastily arranged news conference at Boston Garden. "But the injuries got a hold of me and I couldn't shake 'em."

The announcement came as no great surprise—Bird had fought to overcome a variety of injuries over the past four years. But the moment still carried plenty of attendant emotion. His retirement and the on-again, off-again plans of Earvin Johnson, Jr., Bird's friend and longtime foe with the Los Angeles Lakers, brought to a close the most glorious era in the history of basketball.

Until Bird and Johnson came along in the fall of 1979, the game had struggled to find an identity among American professional sports. But Larry and Earvin changed all that. The public had never seen anything quite like their rivalry. Larry and the Celtics vs. Magic and the Lakers. By 1986, the two had led their teams to three NBA championships apiece, and suddenly the whole world was interested. Or so it seemed.

Thus the age of Camelot.

Bird was the boy wonder who pulled the proverbial sword out of the stone. Celtics president Red Auerbach was a modern version of Merlyn, the gruff old trickster and mentor. And Johnson was simply Magic, the smiling sorcerer and arch-rival. Together, Larry and Earvin ruled the court as if God himself had smiled upon them and designated them to touch the hearts of basketball freaks everywhere.

And so Right became Might. Left wasn't bad either. But the once barren land of pro basketball, where statistics mongers selfishly fought over the spoils, suddenly was transformed into a new kingdom, ruled by the wondrous pass and the unforeseen assist. Larry and Magic used their special vision to craft these plays, to the awe of fans and players alike. They remade pro basketball into a new game.

Ah, Camelot.

It didn't hurt that their days of yore were filled with a complement of honorable and righteous knights, all of whom were brave and trustworthy and armed with an array of low-post moves and jump shots.

They could play, those Celtics and Lakers.

At one time or another, Magic had Kareem Abdul-

Boxing the Doctor

Jabbar, Jamaal Wilkes, James Worthy, Robert McAdoo, Norm Nixon and Michael Cooper alongside him. Bird's Celtics featured Kevin McHale, the Chief, Dennis Johnson, Tiny Archibald, M.L. Carr, Cedric Maxwell, Dave Cowens, Bill Walton and Danny Ainge.

"I think Robert Parish was the best teammate I ever played with and Dennis Johnson was the best player I ever played with," Bird said in praising his band of Celtic brothers. "M.L. Carr was probably the funniest teammate I ever had, and Kevin McHale was the best inside player I've ever seen."

If Bird was their king, Boston Garden was his castle. "Hell," he once quipped, "this is my building."

There on the hallowed parquet, shrouded in that Celtic aura, the boy king wielded his Excalibur, the three-point shot. When he didn't want to go for the heavy metal, he employed his other skills, the deadly passing, the determined rebounding, the soft little hooks, the picks and rolls, the stealthy defense.

So it went in Camelot.

Five times, Larry Legend and his knights went after pro basketball's version of the Holy Grail, the NBA title. Three times they slew the dragons and brought the trophy back to Boston. Twice the dragons scorched them.

But championships weren't the only golden moments in Camelot. Larry personally ensured there were scores of others, many of which rest sweetly today in the memories of fat old armchair Celtics.

Ah, Camelot.

A quick rerun of those days of grandeur should include:

• February 1981 at the Forum in Los Angeles, in the middle of a spirit-breaking road trip. Bird racks up 36 points, 21 rebounds, 5 steals and 6 assists to lead Boston to the win over Magic and the Lakers.

• March 1983, Bird answers a loss to the Pacers in Indiana one night by scoring 53 against them the next night in Boston Garden.

• The 1984 playoffs, Game 7 vs. Bernard King and the Knicks at Boston Garden. Bird's numbers? 12 rebounds, 10 assists and 39 points.

Excalibur

• Game 5 vs. the Lakers in the 1984 NBA Finals. The game was crucial and so was Larry, with 34 points and 17 rebounds. He hit 15 of 20 from the floor.

• The Bourbon Street Blast, in New Orleans against the Atlanta Hawks in March 1985. Bird scores 60, just nine days after McHale had set a new team single-game scoring record with 57.

• Valentine's Day, 1985, when Bird broke hearts in Portland in overtime, totalling 47 points, 14 rebounds and 11 assists.

• The Steal (who doesn't know about this one?) in Game 5 of the 1987 Eastern Finals, when Larry ripped off an Isiah Thomas pass to

feed D.J. for the winning layup.

• Game 7 of the 1988 Eastern semifinals vs. Atlanta, when Dominique Wilkins scored 47 in the Garden, but the Legend finished with 20 in the fourth quarter to drive Boston to the next round.

• The Lazarus Act of 1992, when Bird fought off back pain to score 49 with 12 assists and 14 rebounds in 54 minutes of a triple-overtime win over Portland in the Garden.

LETTING GO

It wasn't easy for Larry to turn loose his grip on such greatness. His wife Dinah had suggested

Mr. Assist

retirement a year earlier. But he persisted, hoping that the back pain would go away. Over the summer, retirement "was in and out of my head," he said. After the Olympic games ended in early August, his deliberations intensified. He spent late nights twisting and turning, trying to decide.

There was hope that he might try to play a 60-game schedule that would diminish his travel. Never a part-time guy, he quickly nixed that option.

"That's not the way I approach things," he explained.

Finally he faced the inevitable, spoke with his doctors and made up his mind.

"Are you sure?" the Celtics' Dave Gavitt asked when Bird informed him of his decision.

He was sure.

"Emotionally, it's very tough for me right now because I'm giving up something I love, something I have been doing for a long time," he said in announcing his retirement. "But I have to give it up. I don't want to go out this way, but I have to."

The emerging reality wasn't easy on Celtics' brass, either. Auerbach was downright grim about future prospects during rookie camp in July. It seemed as if four years of uncertainty over Bird's status had finally worn down the entire organization.

But the press conference was not a time of gloom for Auerbach. Rather, it was a time to celebrate the accomplishments of a great basketball club. Auerbach had constructed three great teams in Boston—the Bill Russell dynasty, the Dave Cowens group and Bird's Camelot. At 75 years of age, it seems a safe bet that Auerbach won't be building too many more great teams. That task has been turned over to Gavitt now.

So Red wasn't just saying goodbye to Larry, he was saying goodbye to a part of himself.

He stepped up first and offered the perspective of his 42 years with what is arguably America's greatest pro sports club. ("If you never played for the Boston Celtics, you never really played professional basketball," Bird said.)

McHale

"I remember when he first came here," Auerbach told the assembly. "He looked like a country bumpkin. But when you looked in his eyes, you knew he was no dummy."

Yet Auerbach admitted that even Bird's eyes didn't reveal just how good he was going to be.

The press asked Bird when he himself knew he was headed for greatness. "It didn't take me long to realize I was going to be a great player in this league," he answered. "I remember the day of rookie camp down in Marshfield. Dave Cowens was there, and Tiny Archibald, and M.L. Carr. It seemed that everyone showed up to see how good I was going to be. The thing is, Rick Robey was covering me, so I thought I was going to be even better than I was."

The laughter rolled through the room, but the media suspected he was masking his feelings.

Bird was asked if he felt sad.

"It's not a sad day," he replied, "but it's a very emotional day. I tried to prepare myself for this, but once you sign the papers that say you've retired, once you get up there and tell the people, it's a little bit different. I've decided to go to a new life, but I'm going to miss this life. I've been on a high for 17 years."

He did admit that he was fighting off tears. "The reason I'm making so many jokes," he confessed, "is to save myself from crying."

Joni Mitchell once wrote that laughing or crying, it's all the same release. So Bird quipped his way through the difficult moments. But across pro basketball, there weren't many belly laughs.

"The Bulls regret this is one of the saddest days in NBA history with the retirement of Larry Bird," said Chicago general manager Jerry Krause in a prepared release.

From the Cleveland Cavaliers, the pronouncements were almost funereal. "We have lost one of the true legends of our time," said center Brad Daugherty.

"The game has lost one of the greatest players of all time," agreed his coach, Lenny Wilkens.

"Pro basketball has just thrown away the mold," Knicks coach Pat Riley said. "He was one of a kind... unique... Not just the best of the best but the only one who did what he did. He was a true warrior."

"It's kind of like when Alexander the Great decided he wasn't going to conquer any more countries," observed Indiana Pacers president Donnie Walsh.

Still, few were truly surprised by the announcement. Bird had played with the "Dream Team" in the 1992 Summer Olympic Games in Barcelona, and while his effort there was inspired, it was also hindered by his back pain.

His Olympic teammates sensed that the games he played with them might be his last. ""When Larry retires, that's it," Magic told reporters during the Olympics. "He'll be gone from the game, and we won't get to see what he does anymore. There were great ones before him, and there'll be great ones after. But there will never, ever, never be another Larry Bird."

"I know the time I spent with Larry on the so-called Dream Team was special," said Chicago's Michael Jordan. "He was one of the greatest players ever and a great leader, and to be able to play with him fulfills one of my dreams."

In his time, Bird had fulfilled the dreams of millions.

"I remember me and DJ would be sitting on the bench at the end of a game," he recalled. "And I'd look up and say, 'I just can't believe 15,000 people would come to watch us play.' I never could understand it. I never will understand it."

Yet Bird did understand. He drew his energy from the Garden crowd and took great pleasure before big games in asking the fans to help boost the Celtics through the tough spots. "All I ask of the fans," he once explained, "is to be vocal, to keep it loud, to pick it up if they see we're a little fatigued and to get us over the hump."

They got each other over the hump, Larry and his fans.

Asked how he wanted to be remembered, Bird quipped, "That he didn't weigh as much as everyone thought he would."

Turning serious, he added, "One thing I know, I played as hard as I could every time I was out there. I wasn't going to let an injury stop me from diving on the floor for a loose ball. I had to compete at a high level. I played one way—as hard as I could—and my body held up pretty well over the years. I played in over 1,100 games. I gave my heart, body and soul for the Celtics. I hope that's how they remember me."

He said he didn't want the fanfare of retirement, but he is eager to see his number "33" hanging in the Garden rafters with the other Celtic greats. Although plans are progressing for a new Boston Garden, Bird said, "I definitely want my number to go up in the old Garden because it's a special place for me."

The Celtics also announced that he would stay with the organization as a special assistant to Gavitt. With his retirement, Bird gave up $3.75 million in salary he was slated to receive for the season, but those close to him say that he has banked $20 million or more over the years. He had once predicted that he would leave Boston someday with every penny he had ever earned. And he had.

"If I had a healthy back now, I'd play for nothing," he said.

No one doubted him.

Yet there was mild surprise in Boston that he didn't immediately pack up and head for Indiana, as he had threatened to do upon retirement.

The Chief in 1981

"For a couple of months, I thought I would sell my home [in Brookline]," he said. "But I can't sell that house. I don't care if I live in it myself or not, but I don't want someone else moving in there who has no idea of the ups and downs. That house has more memories. It's a very special place."

For a special player.

At a special time in the history of the game.

At the end of the press conference, Dave Gavitt stepped back to the rostrum and called for champagne to make one final toast to Larry. He then turned and called for someone to fill a glass for Bird.

"How 'bout a beer?" said the Hick from French Lick, with a grin.

The room broke into a final round of laughter.

Which is just the way he wanted to go out.

"This is the greatest life in the world," he said. "If you know how to play basketball, it's the easiest game in the world. Don't feel sorry for me. I had a great life the last 17 years. I've had nothing but highs."

But Celtics fans everywhere weren't feeling sorry for him. They were feeling sorry for themselves.

Camelot was gone.

"Without Magic and without Bird, I don't think the Celtics-Lakers rivalry will be as intense," said Jim Caton, a Laker fan in Los Angeles. "When we play Boston now, I don't really feel the sense of competition. It's a huge swing from the old dynasties, the Lakers and Boston. The torch has been passed."

Larry and Magic craved championships.

Lords Of The Rings

Between 1979 and 1987, Magic Johnson and Larry Bird introduced hoops to a new phenomenon—mass popularity. The entire sport rose up and sailed to unimagined heights on the wings of their high-flying personal competition.

Their college teams met for the first time in the 1979 NCAA championship game. Bird and Indiana State against Magic and Michigan State. The resulting battle attracted the highest television ratings in the history of the Final Four.

They were merely college athletes, each of them relatively unknown before that season, yet their chemistry was so strong it was nearly tangible. And practically inexplicable. Although television networks have spent millions since then hyping and promoting the NCAA championship, the ratings have never equalled that 1979 game.

Almost from the start of their relationship, Bird and Magic were cast as basketball's Odd Couple. Eventually, the writers would come to describe them as "inextricably linked," but Larry and Magic really didn't care much for each other in the early days of their rivalry.

Magic was a precocious sophomore at Michigan State in 1979, an easygoing kid with dancing eyes and a quick smile. He naturally liked people and was open with reporters and fans alike.

Larry Bird rested somewhere at the other end of the spectrum. He moved through his senior year at Indiana State in a grim silence. He didn't trust reporters and seldom spoke with them. The burden of carrying the

Sycamores seemed to have left him sullen.

Bird was basketball's debatable phenomenon that season as Indiana State ripped through the regular schedule undefeated. Some thought he was a great player headed for the Hall of Fame. Others figured his fame sprang from the Sycamore's second-rate schedule.

Bird, however, settled the debate with his play at the Final Four in Salt Lake City. There, against Mark Aguirre and Depaul in the national semifinals, he registered one of the all-time stellar performances in NCAA tournament history: He made 16 of 19 field goal attempts for 35 points and controlled the boards with 16 rebounds.

Even so, State barely won, 76-74.

With a 33-game unbeaten streak and the top ranking in the national polls, the Sycamores faced one final obstacle—Michigan State.

The media hype for the championship was tremendous.

Magic, affable and black, against Bird, scowling and white.

"To me, it's a serious game," Bird said when asked by reporters about the difference between Magic and himself. "Now you wouldn't expect me to be havin' all kinds of fun when the score's tied, two seconds are left on the clock and the other guys have the ball. It's nice that Magic laughs a lot. I just hope he won't be laughing in my face after he makes a big play."

Michigan State's answer to Bird was a match-up zone. The Indiana State star was snared every way he turned. Hassled into missing 14 of 21 shots, he scored only 19. And while Michigan State found foul trouble early, the Sycamores made only 10 of 22 free throws.

The Spartans led by a dozen in the first half, and in the second, when Indiana State threatened, Michigan State guard Terry Donnelly answered with five long-range jump shots. The Spartans won easily, 75-64. Johnson finished with 24 points and 7 rebounds and was named the Outstanding Player.

Contrary to Bird's fears, Magic was pretty good about keeping his game face affixed. Only after the Spartans had won did he allow himself a smile. Then he went home, got some rest and began pondering his future. Should he turn professional?

Bird, on the other hand, already had his future set out for him. The Celtics had drafted him with the sixth pick of the first round the previous spring (1978). As a fifth-year college player, Bird had been eligible for the draft, and Boston was willing to wait a year for his services. Red Auerbach and Bob Woolf, Bird's agent, dickered over the contract until finally agreeing on a $650,000-per-year deal — then the highest salary ever paid an NBA rookie.

"Now, I don't think I'm worth as much as Bird," Magic said facetiously that spring as he waited to make his decision. "Let's be honest. He's played longer, has got the experience and the accolades and, besides, wow, he's a white superstar. Basketball sure needs him. But think of me in the NBA. One thing I'm always going to do is have fun. There is time for business, time for school and time for fun. You know, things can be happenin' at a party before I get there, but when I show up they just happen more."

Magic decided to join Larry Bird at the NBA party that fall of 1979 (the Lakers made him the top pick in the draft). Just as he had predicted, things started happenin'. Within months of their college clash, these two dynamic players moved in as rookies and assumed the leadership of the league's most storied franchises. In one short season, Larry and Magic virtually transformed the NBA into their personal one-on-one match, while millions of new fans followed the proceedings with fascination.

Yet even with their following, both young players faced numerous questions about their abilities. And both shattered stereotypes every time they played. Larry Bird was white and raised in near poverty in a family torn apart by alcohol abuse. Earvin Johnson was black, the product of a stable middle-class home where both parents worked to provide advantages for their children.

As a player, Johnson was considered a fleet, infinitely talented blue-chipper. In reality, he wasn't much of a jumper and had virtually no outside shot, yet he had honed his skills with endless hours on the playgrounds. The product of his effort was a truly unique big man, fluid enough to play point guard brilliantly.

Bird was considered slow and lead-footed, unable to jump. He even played that angle up a bit that fall of 1979. "I've never considered myself a super athlete," he told reporters. "I admit I'm not the quickest guy in the

Bird shoots out of a triple team in the 1979 NCAA title game.

world. In fact, I'm slow. But I've always tried to make up for that in other ways. I block out and I follow up shots for rebounds. And if there's a loose ball on the floor, I'll be down there bumping heads."

It sounded nice, but in reality, Bird was a marvelously gifted athlete who worked constantly to improve his natural ability. His first real pro test came in a 1979 exhibition game with the Philadelphia 76ers and Julius Erving. Shooting seven of 15 from the field, Bird scored 18 points, but the 'Sixers won easily, 115-90. "I guess the best thing to say is that he can play," Erving commented afterward. "He's what he's supposed to be, what you've read about. You can feel the intensity he has, the moves. He can create his own offense; he was talking all the time out there. I have a very

favorable opinion of him as a player."

The same things, of course, were being said about Magic. Over the coming years, their dual careers would unfold with an almost eerie symmetry. They would continue to mirror each other's experiences and successes and failures. Eventually they would even come to be friends, mainly because they shared one very important trait— an incredible, almost overbearing drive to win, to succeed.

"We're both the same," Johnson said. "We'll do anything to win. You can list all the great players you want, but there are only a couple of winners."

Which is exactly how they inaugurated their pro careers, by winning.

Magic's Los Angeles finished as the top team in the Western Conference in

Bird eyes Magic (Photos courtesy Indiana State)

1980 with a 60-22 record.

Only Bird's Celtics—featuring Dave Cowens and Cedric Maxwell in the frontcourt—bettered that with a 61-21 finish. Bird had averaged 21.5 points and better than 10 rebounds in leading his team to what was then the best turnaround in league history. The year before he arrived, Boston had finished 29-53. That upswing of 32 games resulted in Bird being named rookie of the year.

But the Celtics ran aground against Julius Erving and the Philadelphia 76ers in the Eastern Conference playoff finals and lost 4-1. That June, Bird and his teammates watched Magic and the Lakers claim the world championship, which made for a miserable offseason in Boston.

GREEN TIME

The loss to Philadelphia in the 1980 playoffs taught the Celtics one clear lesson—they had to get bigger. They couldn't battle the 'Sixers' twin towers

of Darryl Dawkins and Caldwell Jones with a front line that ran no taller than 6-9.

As usual, Red Auerbach was ready with a remedy. In 1979, Auerbach had been eager to get rid of Robert McAdoo, the prolific scorer who hadn't fit in with the Celtics. And Detroit Pistons coach Dick Vitale was just as eager to get him, so the Pistons agreed to make a deal. Earlier, the Celtics had signed Detroit's M.L. Carr as a restricted free agent. Thus they owed the Pistons compensation. Accordingly, Auerbach offered to "give up" McAdoo for Detroit's two first-round draft picks in 1980.

For some unimaginable reason, Detroit agreed.

Then the Pistons sweetened the deal by finishing a dreadful last in the NBA for 1980, meaning the Celtics had the number one pick to go with the 13th selection. Auerbach wanted Kevin McHale, a smooth power forward out of the University of Minnesota, but Red and coach Bill

Fitch also wanted veteran center Robert Parish, whom the Golden State Warriors wanted to trade.

The Warriors, who picked third, wanted to draft Joe Barry Carroll out of Purdue and knew they would need the top pick to get him. Thus Auerbach's big deal became a reality. He traded Boston's two picks to Golden State for Parish and the number-three pick in the draft. As a result, Auerbach and Fitch got the frontcourt of the future—Parish at center and McHale at power forward. The Warriors, meanwhile, drafted Carroll first and Rickey Brown thirteenth. The deal was branded the most lopsided trade ever by 19 NBA general managers in a 1989 poll by the *Sporting News*.

"Red has done it again," Bill Fitch declared during a draft-day press conference.

Yet even Fitch didn't know just how badly the big men would be needed. Center Dave Cowens went through Fitch's brutal training camp

Houston's Mike Dunleavy and Gerald Henderson go for a loose ball in Game 1.
(Ron Koch photo)

that fall, then abruptly decided to retire. At first,the season appeared headed toward a personnel disaster. Maxwell, the team's first-round pick in 1977; Archibald, the point guard; and McHale all had contract disputes. All three key players joined the team late, and Boston got off to a slow start.

In time, the team worked out its difficulties and became quite a unit. In the backcourt, Chris Ford started alongside the 6'1" Archibald. The league had just installed its three-point shot in 1979, and Ford quickly acquired the distinction of making the first trey in league history.

A New Yorker, Archibald's instincts had been honed on a Bronx playground. Then he attended Texas-El Paso, and after that was drafted by

the Kansas City Kings, where he was groomed and coached by Bob Cousy. He adopted much of the former Boston great's freewheeling approach to the game. In 1972-73, Archibald had led the league in scoring (34 points per game) and assists (11 per game). But in Boston, his scoring wasn't as important as his play-making. He had a knack for distributing the ball just where Bird wanted it.

"There is nobody better than Tiny," Larry declared.

For the autocratic Fitch, the basketball ideal was a motion offense that wound its way toward an inside bucket. He stressed passing and disciplined patterns of play. Having been an excellent college coach at North Dakota, he liked hard workers

who accepted their roles. Which is exactly how Ford and backup point guard Gerald Henderson approached the game. And M.L. Carr was another in the same mold. In fact, he more than any player came to epitomize the Celtic ideal of team first, strong defense, and heady play. With Cowens' departure, Bird assumed the silent leadership of the team, but it was Carr who supplied the spirit.

The frontcourt had the makings of greatness. Maxwell was at the height of his career, and McHale quickly showed an ability to score and block shots. Plus he was happy to come off the bench. Parish, too, played with pride and grace. He ran the floor and shot his startlingly accurate rainbow jumper, which he had acquired in high school in Shreveport, Louisiana, when his coach made him shoot over an extended broom.

Out of the gate, this group struggled to a 7-5 record, and Bird placed the blame on himself. "Max isn't scoring enough," he said, "and it's my fault, because I should be getting the ball to him. I know how to do it, and I haven't been doing it."

Like Magic with the Lakers, Bird's passing sustained the Celtics. And like Magic, Bird, too, had to learn to keep his teammates involved. That facet of his game improved greatly as the season progressed, and the Celtics grew into an inspiring example of precise ball movement. From their fast breaks to their half-court game, they developed a knack for finding the open man.

Their competition again in the Eastern Conference was the Philadelphia 76ers, who had added an impressive rookie in guard Andrew Toney. The regular-season crown came down to a final meeting between the two teams at Boston Garden, which the Celtics won, 98-94, behind Bird's 24 points. Archibald hit two free throws at the end to get the win, which tied Boston and Philly at 62 wins apiece. The teams had split their series, 3-3, but the tiebreaker gave Boston the home-court advantage in the playoffs.

After a first-round bye, Boston blew past Chicago in the second round, setting up another meeting with

Carr and Parish surround Malone in the 1981 Finals. (Koch photo)

Philadelphia in the Eastern finals. The Celtics felt confident and ready. Then, just like that, they lost their first game at home, captured the second and lost two more in Philadelphia. Suddenly, they had fallen behind, 3-1, and were facing a repeat of 1980, when the 'Sixers moved them aside, 4-1.

Fitch told them he had been associated with only one team that had ever come back from a 3-1 deficit, but he felt this team could do it.

"I'm telling you, it was the most rewarding experience a group of guys can have in this sport," he said.

They responded by trailing 59-49 at halftime of the fifth game in the Garden. In the locker room, Fitch made one more appeal, this time a shouting one. He said he didn't mind losing but he did mind seeing them play passively.

They worked hard over the next two quarters, but with 1:51 to go, the 'Sixers led by six and Boston's season seemed over. Then Maxwell blocked Andrew Toney's shot, and Archibald took the ball to the other end, where he scored and drew the foul for a three-point play. Like that, the lead was three, 109-106.

The 'Sixers tried to inbound the ball, but Boston's defense forced them to call two timeouts. When they did attempt to make the pass, Bird stole it and scored, cutting the lead to one. Then Carr got another steal and drew a foul. He hit both shots to give Boston the lead, 110-109. Bobby Jones got a shot for Philly, but Parish hampered it. Carr rebounded and was fouled again, enabling Boston to survive, 111-109.

The Celtics, though, didn't have much reason to celebrate. They trailed 3-2 and were headed to the Spectrum for Game 6. Boston hadn't won in Philly in the 11 games they had played there during Bird's pro career.

Their failure seemed a sure bet in the first half, as the 'Sixers went up by 12. Then in the second half, Maxwell got involved in a brouhaha with the Philly fans under one of the baskets. The Boston bench came to his aid, and when order was restored, Maxwell went to work, scoring and rebounding like a madman. Late in the game, Boston had the ball and the

The Bird form

lead, 96-95, when Bird took a 20-footer as the shot clock ran down. The ball hit the rim, rose up and fell back through, 98-95. Toney raced back upcourt with the ball and shot in the lane, but McHale blocked it. Moments later, Maxwell would hit two free throws to keep Boston alive, 100-98.

Game 7 was another fight. Philly led by 11 late in the second half and was still up, 89-83, with 4:34 on the game clock. The Celtics rushed back to tie it at 89, and seconds later Bird came up with a loose ball. He rushed upcourt, looked off to his right, then fired up an 18-foot bank shot. Good! That was momentum enough. Philly

added a free throw, but Boston held on, 91-90, to seal another great comeback.

"There was no one else in the world I wanted to have the ball but me," Bird said later of his last shot. With it, he had sent his team to the Finals.

Out west, Magic and the Lakers had fallen on hard times. He had suffered a cartilege tear in his knee during the season, then struggled back from surgery to rejoin his team late in the schedule. But they never got time to jell. Instead, they lost to Moses Malone and a plodding Houston Rockets team, 2-1, in the opening round. Houston had finished a mediocre 40-

42 in the regular season, after spending the year trying to be a running team. But a late season loss to Boston convinced coach Del Harris that he needed to slow the approach to Malone's pace. After dumping the Lakers, the Rockets whipped San Antonio and Kansas City to meet Boston for the championship.

The Rockets backcourt featured Mike Dunleavy, Calvin Murphy, and Allen Leavell. Robert Reid was a smooth swing player, while Rudy Tomjanovich and Billy Paultz helped Malone up front.

Houston had lost the previous dozen games to the Celtics. But Malone, who averaged nearly 28 points and 15 rebounds, declared that the Celtics were chumps. Game 1 in Boston Garden was surprisingly tight. Houston led 57-51 at the half. Late in the fourth period, with Boston struggling, Bird came upcourt and put up an 18-footer from the right side. As soon as he let it go, he knew it was bad and rushed to the rebound. He caught the ball in mid air as his momentum carried him past the baseline. In an instant, he switched to his left hand (a right-handed shot would have hit the side of the backboard) and swished a 12-footer. The crowd went nuts, with Auerbach leading the cheers. Bill Russell, who was broadcasting the game for CBS, looked on in disbelief. "Larry was able to make the play," Russell said, "because he not only knew where the ball was going to land—he knew that he knew."

The shot carried Boston to a 98-95 win and left Auerbach puffing another cigar. "It was the one best shot I've ever seen a player make," he said afterward.

"Bird sort of flipped it," Houston's Robert Reid said. "What can you say about a play like that?"

After playing on emotion for four straight games, Boston came out flat for Game 2. Fitch was so infuriated he put his fist through a blackboard in the locker room at half time. That did little good, though. Houston's precision and Malone's inside play and rebounding kept the game close. Then the Rockets stole it at the end, 91-90.

Cedric Maxwell was the Finals MVP in 1981.

"Sometimes a slap in the face wakes you up," Carr said.

Duly awakened, they responded with a 94-71 blowout of the Rockets in the Summit. Maxwell did much of the work for Boston, as Reid held Bird to just eight points.

Harris used just six players in Game 4, and Houston again held Bird to eight. Malone ruled the inside, and Houston got a 91-86 win that evened the series at 2-all. Afterward, Malone told the writers he could get four guys off the streets of Petersburg, Virginia, his hometown, and beat the Celtics. "I don't think they're all that good," he said. "I don't think they can stop us from doing what we want to do."

It was just the emotional spark the Celtics needed. "The man threw down a challenge," Maxwell replied, "and this is a team that responds well to challenges."

With Maxwell leading, they took

Game 5 in Boston, 109-80, for a 3-2 lead.

"The Celtics are still chumps," Malone said afterward.

The series returned to Houston that Thursday night, May 14, where Bird broke out of his slump. Boston had a six-point lead at the half and kept it down the stretch. When Houston pulled close late in the fourth, Bird came downcourt and canned his only 3-pointer of the series, which sent Boston on to a 102-91 win and the team's 14th championship.

Afterward in the locker room, Bird stole Auerbach's lit cigar and puffed impishly.

"We're the champions," he said as he broke into a coughing spell.

"He's just one of a kind," Fitch said.

Or maybe two of a kind. The other half of the odd couple was stewing in Los Angeles for another chance at the ring.

The Celtics lineup against the Lakers in '85.

The Laker Girls were Celtics busters in '85.

Bird inside against Jamaal Wilkes.

Showdown

For four seasons, they danced around each other in the NBA, meeting only twice each year in regular-season games. Still, Larry and Magic were always aware of each other. They searched the headlines and kept their eyes on the standings and the box scores. That, of course, was no way for two great players and two great teams to decide who was best. They needed to meet in the Finals.

"Championship rings, I live for them things," Bird would say.

Magic did, too.

Obviously, the Celtics and Lakers needed a showdown. The fans wanted it, the players wanted it, and finally it happened. On three glorious occasions in the mid 1980s, Magic and the Lakers met Bird and the Celtics in the Finals. Across America, it was portrayed as a clash of symbols. East vs. West. Tradition vs. New Wave. Hollywood vs. Beantown. Showtime vs. Shamrocks. Celtic Pride vs. L.A. Cool.

"It's like the opening of a great play," Lakers General Manager Jerry West told the writers just before the 1984 Finals. "Everyone's waiting to see it."

The media hype was tremendous. But beneath all the symbols and media, at the heart of everything, were two guys with immense confidence, supreme talent, and a mutual desire to dominate.

"With Magic, it's a macho thing," West explained. "He wants to be better than everybody else."

The same was true with Bird. "The number one thing is desire," he said, "the ability to do the things you have to do to become a basketball player. I don't think you can teach anyone desire. I think it's a gift. I don't know why I have it, but I do."

As Magic once explained, "I only know how to play two ways. That's reckless and abandon."

And that's how they approached their championship bash. Reckless and abandon. Two forces of pride and ego colliding. In retrospect, the NBA can be ever so thankful that they did. The Boston/ Los Angeles fling in the Finals provided the juice for the league's resurgence. Over Larry's and Magic's first dozen years in the NBA, television rights money alone zoomed from roughly $20 million per year to more than $220 million. In 1990, the NBA's annual revenues totalled an estimated $700 million. "There's no question that Bird and Magic together, with the rivalry they brought us, was an important factor," Russ Granick, the NBA's executive vice president, said during the 1980s.

In sports bars, living rooms and cocktail lounges across America, their competition spawned a running debate as to who was the greatest. Boston claimed a brassy win in

Two for the long run.

The '84 Finals was a collision of legends.

1984, and Bird followed that up with two more years of superior regular-season play, resulting in his being named the league MVP for three consecutive seasons, 1984-86. On the heels of that, Auerbach went so far as to declare him the greatest basketball player ever, greater even than Bill Russell, who had won an unprecedented five MVP awards.

"All I know," Bird said in reply, "is that people tend to forget how great the older great players were. It'll happen that way with me, too." His winning of a third consecutive league MVP award placed him in a category with Russell and Wilt Chamberlain, the only other players to receive the honor three consecutive times. "I'm proud to be in a group with Bill Russell," Bird said in accepting the award. "But Wilt Chamberlain talks a little bit too much for me."

Yet even as Bird claimed his awards, plenty of observers, including Chamberlain, thought Johnson was being shortchanged. "I don't know if there's ever been a better player than Magic," Wilt said.

Bird himself readily agreed. "He's the perfect player," he said of Magic.

Still the debate rolled on. Magic took his team to three championships in four years from 1985 to 1988, including the first back-to-back titles (in '87 and '88) since Russell and the Celtics had last done it in 1969.

The Lakers' success resulted in Magic winning three league MVP awards. Which only renewed the questions. Who was better? Certainly there was no real answer, because greatness can't be measured. It can only be felt. And according to the Celtics and Lakers of the 1980s, it felt pretty good.

LAKER AGONY

Things had gone awry for the Boston Celtics after their 1981 title. They kept adding quality players and kept looking better and better on paper. But on court they still lacked something. In the fall of 1981 they had obtained Danny Ainge, the former Brigham Young guard who had decided to play pro baseball with the Toronto Blue Jays. Boston had

D.J. became a quick factor in '84.

wrestled Ainge away from the Blue Jays in a court battle. Then the Celtics had traded for backup point guard Quinn Buckner and a smooth-shooting former all-star forward, Scott Wedman. The only problem with these acquisitions was the ensuing traffic jam. Where and when would they all play? It wasn't an easy question to answer. When Milwaukee swept Boston in the 1983 playoffs, Red Auerbach decided it was time for yet more changes.

Just weeks after the season ended, Bill Fitch resigned and was promptly replaced by assistant K.C. Jones. The two coaches had had their tiffs during Fitch's four-year tenure in Boston. Fitch's autocratic approach didn't allow much input from K.C., leaving the assistant openly frustrated at times. Jones approached the task of head coach from a completely different perspective than his predecessor. Jones was a players' coach. Where Fitch was a practice monster who spent hours reviewing videotape and expected his players to do the same,

Jones was more laid back, less insistent. Practices were important with Jones, but he favored a relaxed setting. Most of all, he wanted the complete effort from his players at game time, and as the record would reveal, he usually got it.

Jones had been through a rough time since being fired as Washington's head coach after the 1976 season. He had bounced around as an assistant coach and had developed something of a drinking problem. But by the time he became the Celtics boss, he had exorcised those demons and was quite up to the task. Time would prove him the perfect coach for a veteran team.

"I think everyone is more at ease," Cedric Maxwell said when asked about having Jones as the head coach. "We have older players on this team. We know what we can do without being chastised or scolded."

Jones's promotion roughly paralleled another major development in Boston. That August of 1983, Celtics owner Harry Manguerian sold the

team for $15 million to a group headed by Gulf and Western executive Donald Gaston and Alan Cohen, a former Nets executive. It was the twelfth ownership change that Red Auerbach had witnessed in three and a half decades with the team. As with the previous changes, Auerbach remained in firm control of the basketball operations.

Despite the ownership turnover, Auerbach made another big change heading into the 1983-84 season—the acquisition of guard Dennis Johnson from Phoenix for center Rick Robey. The Celtics needed a big defensive guard to match up against Sidney Moncrief in Milwaukee and Andrew Toney in Philadelphia, and the 6'4" Johnson fit just that bill. The move surprised observers because Johnson had been branded as difficult and a troublemaker in both Seattle, where he had helped lead the Sonics to the '79 championship, and in Phoenix, where he had helped lift the Suns to the next level of competitiveness. Seattle coach Lenny Wilkens had gone so far as to label Johnson "a cancer" on the team.

Auerbach, though, figured Johnson would fit in well with Boston's veteran club. He was paired in the backcourt with Gerald Henderson, which gave the Celtics an excellent defensive look. They also had Ainge, Buckner and M.L. Carr off the bench, making for a deep, solid rotation.

But then, as now, Boston's strength was its frontcourt. Cedric Maxwell started at power forward with Parish at center and Bird at the other corner. Off the bench came McHale, Wedman and backup center Greg Kite. There were no thin spots.

Carr and Maxwell provided their usual megadoses of spirit and banter. "Cedric was real funny," Gerald Henderson said. "Our whole team was cocky. But he was our team comedian. Him and M.L. We had a good time. It was all kiddin' around. But when the time came to get serious and win basketball games, we got serious."

"That team," Carr said of the '83-84 Celtics, "talked more junk than any team in the history of the game."

This atmosphere brought a rise in the level of Bird's play. The loss to Milwaukee the previous spring had provided him with a new surge of motivation. He had taken the setback personally. "It's the toughest thing that ever happened in Celtic history," he said afterward. "I'll tell you one thing, I'm going to play more basketball than ever this summer. People say, 'As Larry Bird goes, so go the Celtics.' So okay, next season I'll take on that pressure. I'll come back with more desire than ever. If it's got to start somewhere, it might as well start here."

And so it did. The evolution of his game spun even faster that season, bringing a fusion of increasingly diverse elements, a factor that would set him apart from most other players. The one move that came closest to emerging as his signature was the step back, a moving away from the defender to create shooting or driving room. He became just as well known for his developed ambidexterity and his passing style. Prominent in his portfolio was a capacity for making

Boston whipped Philly to gain the '84 Finals.

freakish plays seem common. He produced them almost nightly.

Despite his often-mentioned lack of leaping ability, Bird's positioning, timing and strong hands made him an ideal rebounder. And his offense had a hauteur to it, particularly when he could make a play at a crucial moment to kill the spirit of an opponent. Around the league, Bird became known for his heartlessness.

"Look in his eyes," Atlanta's Dominique Wilkins once said, "and you see a killer."

"I guess I try to carry myself in a certain way on the court," Bird said of his hauteur. "It's funny because nobody else in my family is like that. It's not that I don't have respect for

my opponents. When you lose that, you've got nothing. But tradition is important here, acting like a Celtic."

"There's so many factors involved with him," K.C. Jones said of Bird. "People don't see everything he does. He's such a hard-nosed competitor and very determined. You don't see superstars like him going after loose balls—especially in pre-season games. His effort is always there."

While other forwards could score, none could match Bird as a passer. In the negotiations for Bird's rookie contract, agent Bob Woolf had argued that as a dominant player Bird was worth $1 million per year. Auerbach attempted to counter that centers, occasionally guards, dominated NBA

Celebration '84

play, but never forwards, never from the corner of the floor. But as his game developed Bird's passing came to demoralize opponents almost as much as his three-point shot. "I grew up all of a sudden," he once said of his adolescence. "I was a guard as a sophomore and junior in high school, before I grew up. And we had some great shooters. I tried to get the ball to the great shooters. Passing is so much part of basketball it's unbelievable. It don't matter who scores the points. It's who gets the ball to the scorer."

With his motivation and his background, Larry Bird came to be something of a basketball force in the mid 1980s. It helped, of course, that he was encased as the centerpiece of a great franchise. From top to bottom, the Celtics displayed an arrogant fierceness. When an October 1983 exhibition game between the 'Sixers and Celtics erupted into a melee, Red Auerbach charged onto the court, took off his glasses and taunted Moses Malone: "I'm not big, hit me." Auerbach, 66 at the time, was later fined $2,500 for his actions. But the mood had been set for the Celtics'

M.L. Carr was one of Bird's favorites.

Maxwell was a factor in '84.

season, and it was decidedly aggressive.

As a player, Jones had been a defensive mind, and that carried over to his coaching approach. He studied opposing players and had a knack for identifying weaknesses. While the rest of the league was thinking of defense in terms of steals and flashy plays, Jones was building a team mentality.

"We used to just flat-out stop people," Henderson said.

They would shut them down at one end and burn them at the other, then snicker while running back downcourt. That act gave them a league-best 62 wins over the course of the regular season. With each victory, their overbearing confidence increased, which was fortunate because they would need it in the playoffs.

The Celtics brushed by Washington in the first round only to run into major problems with Bernard King and the Knicks in the Eastern semifinals. Finally they vanquished New York in seven games and enjoyed a thorough 4-1 whipping of Milwaukee in the conference finals.

Shortly thereafter, Los Angeles finished off the Phoenix Suns and

Larry had supreme confidence.

Kareem and Larry fight for the rebound.

took the Western Conference title. Like the Celtics, the Lakers had been through some changes. They had been swept by Philadelphia in the 1983 Finals, which left General Manager Jerry West figuring ways for a quick reshuffle. Finally during the 1983-84 preseason, he sent Norm Nixon and reserve Eddie Jordan to the San Diego Clippers for backup center Swen Nater and the draft rights to rookie guard Byron Scott, out of Arizona State. In short time, the 6'4" Scott worked into the Laker backcourt, and Showtime would be off and running again.

With injuries and other problems, they had finished the regular season at 54-28. Magic had missed 13 games early in the schedule with an injured finger. Then in February, Jamaal Wilkes had contracted an intestinal infection that hampered him the remainder of the season. Still, the year had held its special moments. Abdul-Jabbar first broke Chamberlain's record for career field goals, then for career scoring when he picked up his 36,420th point against the Utah Jazz. Although he was no longer as dominant as he had once been, Kareem still gave the Lakers a formidable half-court game when they needed it.

Beyond that, James Worthy had quietly come into his own as a forward. He had brilliant quickness, and once Magic got him the ball in the low post, the result was usually a score. He took delight in faking one way then exploding another. And he continued to add range to his shot, building his consistency from 15 feet out.

The Lakers also continued to get good frontcourt minutes and scoring from Robert McAdoo. In the backcourt, Michael Cooper had found his identity as a defensive and three-point specialist, while third-year guard Mike McGee contributed 9.8 points per game.

Once Magic put his finger injury behind him, they rolled along, right through the early rounds of the playoffs. As the Finals opened, there was a sense that Los Angeles was the better team. "The Lakers are more talented than we are," K.C. Jones said.

From the Laker perspective, the situation was laced with tension. It had been 15 years since Los Angeles had last faced Boston in the Finals, yet the numbers were on everyone's mind. Seven times the Lakers had met the Celtics for the championship, and seven times the Lakers had lost.

Hours before Game 1, Kareem was wracked by one of the migraine headaches that had troubled him throughout his career. Team trainer Jack Curran worked the center's neck and back an hour before game time, at one point popping a vetebrae into place. That seemed to do the trick on the 37-year-old captain. He walked out and treated the Garden crowd to 32 points, eight rebounds, five assists, two blocks and a steal. He made 12 of his 17 shots from the floor and eight of nine free throws. He did all of that only when the Lakers slowed down. They spent the rest of the time running their break in one door and out another for a 115-109 win.

Kaput went Boston's home-court edge.

Game 2 then became a James Worthy showcase, at least for the first 47 minutes or so. He hit 11 of 12 from the floor and scored 29 points. Even better, the Lakers had come from behind to take a 115-113 lead with 18 seconds left. McHale went to the free throw line for two shots but missed both. Thoughts of a sweep crossed Boston minds. But the Lakers picked that particular moment for a snooze. Pat Riley had told Magic to call timeout if McHale made the shots. But Magic misunderstood and called timeout after the misses, which gave Boston time to set up the defense. Inbounding at mid court, Magic tossed the ball to Worthy, who spied Byron Scott across the court and attempted to get the ball to him. Lurking in the background praying for just such an opportunity was Henderson. He stepped in, snatched the fat pass and loped down the court for the lay-in. The game was tied, but again Magic made a mistake. He allowed the clock to run down without attempting a final shot.

"The other players never did anything to help him," Riley said later in defense of Magic. "They stood out

As a player, Jones had been a defensive mind, and that carried over to his coaching approach. He studied opposing players and had a knack for identifying weaknesses.

on the perimeter and didn't get open. Kareem moved with 12 seconds left, which meant he was open too early. Magic got blamed."

Late in overtime, Henderson found Wedman on the baseline and got him the ball. From there, the reserve forward put down the key jumper to give Boston a 124-121 win and a 1-1 tie in the series.

"I guess what I'll be remembered for in my career is that steal," Henderson said. "People mention it to me all the time. But even in that same game, in overtime, I like the play where I set up Scott Wedman to make the winning jumper. That goes unnoticed, but I appreciate that play more than the steal. Those were the two points that won the game."

Pat Riley's memory, however, was fixed on the steal. "What will I remember most from this series?" he asked rhetorically afterward. "Simple. Game 2. Worthy's pass to Scott. I could see the seams of the ball, like it was spinning in slow motion, but I couldn't do anything about it."

However deep their

The Celtic starters in '84 were Bird, Maxwell, Parish, Henderson and Johnson.

Bird vs. Cooper

disappointment, the Lakers quickly recovered back home in the Forum. Magic had a Finals record 21 assists, and Showtime rolled to a 137-104 win. Bird was outraged at Boston's flat performance. "We played like a bunch of sissies," he said afterward. "I know the heart and soul of this team, and today the heart wasn't there, that's for sure. I can't believe a team like this would let L.A. come out and push us around like they did. Today I didn't feel we played hard. We got beat bad, and it's very embarrassing."

The next day the Los Angeles papers began touting Worthy as the series MVP, infuriating the Boston players. None was angrier than Dennis Johnson, who had scored only four points in Game 3. "I thought I was into the game," he said, "but Game 3 convinced me I wasn't. Even K.C. had to come over and ask what was wrong. I told him whatever it was, it wouldn't be there again. It was a case of getting mentally and physically aggressive."

The same was true for the entire team. Jones adjusted the team's defense, switching D.J. to cover Magic, and they went back at it. The Lakers took an early lead and seemed poised to again run off with the game. From the bench, Carr vociferously lobbied for the Celtics to become more physical. McHale complied in the second quarter when he clotheslined Kurt Rambis on a breakaway, causing a ruckus under the basket. The incident awakened the Celtics and gave the Lakers reason to pause.

Later, Riley would call the Celtics "a bunch of thugs."

Maxwell, on the other hand, was overjoyed. "Before Kevin McHale hit Kurt Rambis, the Lakers were just running across the street whenever they wanted," he said. "Now they stop at the corner, push the button, wait for the light and look both ways."

Still, Los Angeles held a five-point lead with less than a minute to play in regulation. But Parish stole a bad pass from Magic, and the Laker point guard later missed two key free throws, allowing the Celtics to force an overtime. Late in the extra period, Worthy faced a key free throw. But

McHale, the inside force

Carr hooted loudly from the bench that he would miss. Worthy did, and Maxwell stepped up and greeted him with the choke sign. The Celtics vaulted to a 129-125 win to tie the series again and regain the homecourt edge.

The free throw misses and the turnover would trouble Magic for a long time. "I thought the free throws more than the pass were mistakes," he said later. "Those were things I—not the team—I should have taken care of. When you miss the shots you go home and sit in the dark."

The Celtics realized they were on to something. The Lakers could be intimidated. "We had to go out and make some things happen," Henderson recalled of Game 4. "If being physical was gonna do it, then we had to do it. I remember in the fourth game that was the turnaround. We had to have that game or we were gonna be down 3-1. We had to have it. We had guys who could make some things happen."

Dennis Johnson was certainly one

of those guys. After struggling early in the series, he would finish the final four games by scoring 22, 22, 20 and 22 points.

Boston Globe writer Bob Ryan had seen Bird perform in many situations but listed the fifth game of that '84 series as his favorite. "The so-called 'heat game' in 1984," he said. "The fifth game with Los Angeles. It was 97 degrees in the Boston Garden, and the one player that you could have predicted turned this game into a positive was Larry Bird. That sums up Larry Bird. The Lakers were sitting there sucking on oxygen and Bird is saying, 'Hey, we've all played outdoors in the summer. We've all played on asphalt. We've all done this. Why should this be different? It's just because we have uniforms on and it's a national television audience.'"

In that crucial match, Bird was 15 for 20 from the floor for 34 points as Boston won, 121-103. Kareem, meanwhile, had appeared to be just what he was, a 37-year-old man running in sweltering heat. How hot was it? a reporter asked.

"I suggest," Kareem replied, "that you go to a local steam bath, do 100 pushups with all your clothes on, and then try to run back and forth for 48 minutes. The game was in slow motion. It was like we were running in mud."

"I love to play in the heat," Bird said, smiling. "I just run faster, create my own wind."

"He was just awesome," Riley said of Bird. "He made everything work."

But it wasn't just Bird. The Celtics were a full-blown team. "This is probably the best game we ever played," D.J. said.

The Lakers then answered the Celtics' aggressiveness in Game 6 back in the air-conditioned Forum. In the first period, Worthy shoved Maxwell into a basket support. From there, the Lakers rode their newfound toughness and an old standby. Kareem scored 30, and Los Angeles pulled away down the stretch for a 119-108 win to tie the series at three apiece. As Carr left the Forum floor, a fan pitched a cup of liquid in his face, enraging the Celtics. Carr said afterward that the Lakers had declared "all-out war." Bird

Running the floor was something Bird did surprisingly well in the early years.

suggested that the Lakers wear their hard hats for Game 7 in the Garden.

The entire city of Boston was juiced up for the event that Tuesday night June 12. The Lakers needed a police escort to get from their hotel to North Station, the subway station adjoining the Garden. Carr came out wearing goggles to mock Kareem and told the Lakers they weren't going to win. Not in the Garden.

Maxwell further ensured that, telling his teammates to put the load on his back because he was ready to carry them. Which he did. He presented a high-action low-post puzzle that the Lakers never solved. He demoralized them on the offensive boards. He drew fouls. By halftime, he had made 11 of 13 free throws. When they tried to double-team him, he passed them silly. He finished with 24 points, eight assists and eight rebounds. Bird had 20 points and 12

rebounds, Parish 14 points and 16 rebounds. And D.J. was majestic again with 22 points.

Even against that barrage, the Lakers fought back from a 14-point deficit to trail by just three with more than a minute left. Magic had the ball, but D.J. knocked it loose. Michael Cooper recovered it for L.A. Magic again went to work and spied Worthy open under the basket. But before Magic could make the pass, Maxwell knocked the ball away yet again. Later the vision of Worthy open under the basket would haunt Magic.

At the other end, D.J. drew a foul and made the shots, spurring the Celtics to their fifteenth championship, 111-102. Bird was named the MVP after averaging 27.4 points, 14 rebounds, 3.2 assists and 2 steals over the series. But Maxwell's seventh-game performance had been incredible. And once again Dennis

Johnson had delivered in the clutch.

All of which was celebrated deliriously by the Garden crowd. "We worked hard for this," Bird said afterward. "Anybody gonna say we didn't earn it?"

Auerbach enjoyed yet another of his very fat, very special cigars as Commissioner David Stern presented the league trophy. The Celtics president clutched it with satisfaction and asked, "What ever happened to that Laker dynasty I've been hearing so much about?"

SHOWTIME

Unfortunately, the Lakers couldn't get out of town after the 1984 Finals. They had to spend one more night in their hotel, trapped inside of Boston with the Celtic blues again. Needless to say, it was a sleepless night. Owner Jerry Buss chainsmoked. Michael

Parish gave the Celtics a championship presence in the post.

Cooper spent the time in deep and miserable mourning sequestered in his room with his wife Wanda. Pat Riley just wished he had a reason to diagram tomorrow's plays, anything to fight the insomnia.

Magic Johnson was joined by his two friends, Isiah Thomas of the Detroit Pistons and Mark Aguirre of the Dallas Mavericks. "We talked until the morning came," Thomas said later, "but we never talked about the game much. For that one night I think I was his escape from reality."

The pain would remain for months. Magic returned to California, where he was set to move into his new Bel-Air mansion, only the furniture hadn't arrived. His palace sat as empty as his heart. So he hid out for three days in his Culver City apartment. His mother,

Christine, phoned to see how he was doing. He told her he just couldn't talk about it.

Yet everywhere he turned, there seemed to be something to read about it. The Celtics were having fun with their victory. McHale even dubbed him "Tragic Johnson." Asked about the 1984-85 season, Bird said of the Lakers, "I'd like to give them the opportunity to redeem themselves. I'm sure they have guys who feel they didn't play up to their capabilities." Asked if he meant Magic, Bird replied, "You think we don't love it? Magic's having nightmares [about his poor play]."

Magic retorted that he had no need for redemption.

Even worse than the Celtic cockiness was the trashing he took

from the L.A. newspapers. "I sat back when it was over," he said later, "and I thought, 'Man, did we just lose one of the great playoff series of all time, or didn't we?' This was one of the greatest in history. Yet all you read was how bad I was."

Despite the sauciness between Bird and Magic, their relationship warmed that summer when they made a sneaker commercial for Converse, the shoe manufacturer they represented. Their competition, however, remained as intense as ever that next season. At age 28, Bird flexed his talent during the regular season, averaging 28.7 points, 10.5 rebounds and 6.6 assists per game. The Celtics, though, were not as strong. Henderson had held out for more money over the summer, so Boston traded him to Seattle. General Manager Jan Volk explained that the team figured Danny Ainge had progressed enough to carry the starting load. Yet there was no doubt the trade left the Celtics thin. Maxwell, too, had held out for more money, and the Celtics eventually came up with a new contract. But during the season, the power forward was troubled by chronic knee problems that eventually required exploratory surgery. In his absence, McHale moved from sixth man to starter. The Celtic starters—Bird, McHale, Johnson, Ainge and Parish— averaged better than 2,500 minutes of playing time over the season.

The Lakers, on the other hand, had come back with a fierceness and were once again a deep, talented team. By playoff time, the frontcourt was bolstered by the return of Mitch Kupchak and Jamaal Wilkes to go with Kareem, Worthy, Rambis, McAdoo and Larry Spriggs. The backcourt showed Magic, Scott, Cooper and McGee. As a group, the Lakers were driven by their '84 humiliation.

"Those wounds from last June stayed open all summer," Riley said as the playoffs neared. "Now the misery has subsided, but it never leaves your mind completely. Magic is very sensitive to what people think about him, and in his own mind I think he heard those questions over and over again to the point where he began to rationalize and say, 'Maybe I do have to concentrate more.' I think the whole experience has made him grow up in a lot of ways."

After all, Johnson was a mere 25, and at a time when most pro players were just beginning to feel comfortable in the game, he already owned two championship rings. Across pro basketball observers sensed that he was about to add to his jewelry collection. The Celtics, however, were conceding nothing. With a 63-19 regular-season finish, they had again claimed the home-court advantage. The Lakers had finished 62-20. And neither team dallied in the playoffs. Boston dismissed Cleveland, Detroit and Philadelphia in quick succession. The Lakers rolled past Phoenix, Portland and Denver.

For the first time in years, the Finals returned to a 2-3-2 format, with the first two games in Boston, the middle three in Los Angeles, and the last two, if necessary, back in Boston. The situation set up an immense opportunity for the Lakers to steal one in the Garden, then pressure the Celtics back in Los Angeles. However it would be done, Magic, Kareem and company figured on rectifying their humiliation from 1984.

Little did they know they would have to suffer one final, profound embarrassment. Game 1 opened on Memorial Day, Monday May 27, with both teams cruising on five days rest. The Lakers, however, quickly took on the appearance of guys who had just come off two weeks on the graveyard shift. The 38-year-old Abdul-Jabbar, in particular, slogged up and down the court, while Robert Parish seemed to glide. Often Kareem would just be reaching the top of the key to catch up, when all of a sudden the action raced the other way. He finished the day with 12 points and three rebounds. And Magic had only one rebound. Meanwhile, the famed Showtime running game was slowed to a belly crawl.

And the Celtics?

They placed a huge red welt on the Lakers' scar from the previous year, 148-114. Scott Wedman hit 11 for 11 from the floor, including four three-pointers. Danny Ainge sank six straight buckets at the end of the first quarter to finish the period with 15 points. "It was one of those days," K.C. Jones said, "where if you turn around and close your eyes, the ball's gonna go in."

For all their success, the Celtics suddenly quieted their trash talking, as if they sensed that they had gone too far. They hadn't expected it to be this easy. And the last thing they wanted to do was rile the Lakers. "It's definitely time to back off," Maxwell said. "It's not like backgammon or cribbage, where if you beat someone bad enough you get two wins."

But it was too late. The teams didn't play again until Thursday, and there was an uneasy air in Boston despite the big win.

The next morning in the Lakers' film sessions, Kareem moved to the front row, rather than recline in the farther reaches as he usually did. And he didn't blink when Riley ran and reran the gruesome evidence of his terrible performance. In fact, the captain went to each of his teammates later and personally apologized for his effort.

"He made a contract with us that it would never happen again. Ever," Riley said later. "That game was a blessing in disguise. It strengthened the fiber of this team. Ever since then, Kareem had this look, this air about him."

Before Game 2 on Thursday, Kareem went to Riley and asked if his father, Al Alcindor, could ride on the team bus to the Garden. Riley consented and then thought of his own father, Lee, who had been a minor league baseball manager. Just before he died, the elder Riley had told his son that someday he would have to make a stand, that someday he would have to kick some butt. Riley recalled those words to his players in his pre-game talk.

It was time, he said, to make a stand.

And they did. Kareem, in particular, reasserted himself with 30 points, 17 rebounds, eight assists and three blocks. Cooper hit eight of nine from the floor to finish with 22 points. And like that, the Lakers evened the series, 109-102. Best of all, they had stolen a game in the Garden and now returned to the Forum for three straight.

"They expected us to crawl into a hole," Lakers assistant Dave Wohl said of the Celtics. "It's like the bully on the block who keeps taking your lunch money every day. Finally you get tired of it and you whack him."

They hosted the Celtics on Sunday afternoon and really whacked 'em again, returning the favor of Game 1, 136-111. The Lakers ran away in the second half, during which Kareem became the league's all-time leading playoff scorer with 4,458 points.

Bird, meanwhile, had fallen into a two-game shooting slump, going 17 for 42. He had been troubled by a chronically sore right elbow and bad back, although some speculated his real trouble was Cooper's defense.

Bird connected with Chief

Bird confirmed as much by refusing to offer excuses.

As with '84, the series was marked by physical play, although this time around it seemed to be the Lakers who were determined to gain an intimidation edge. "We're not out to physically harm them," Kareem offered. "But I wouldn't mind hurting their feelings." Before Game 4, the NBA's vice president of operations, Scotty Stirling, warned each coach that fighting and extra rough play would be met with fines and suspensions. Riley told his players of Stirling's warning, but K.C. Jones chose not to. With their uninhibited play, the Celtics gained an edge, and the close game came down to one final Celtic possession. Bird had the ball but faced a double-team, so he dumped it off to D. J. above the foul line. From there,

Johnson drilled the winner with two seconds left. Boston had evened the series, 107-105.

Game 5 two nights later in the Forum was the critical showdown. McHale answered the call for Boston, putting down 16 early points and forcing Riley to make a defensive switch in the second period. The L.A. coach put Kareem on McHale and left the shorter Rambis to contend with Parish. It worked immediately. Kareem scored 36, as the Lakers walked away with a 3-2 lead, 120-111.

From there it went back to Boston. Jerry West didn't dare make the trip for fear of spooking the proceedings. Across the country old Lakers held their breath and watched the tube. After eight painful losses, this seemed to be the best chance yet to end Boston's domination. The Celtics

would have to win the final two games. With a mere 38 hours rest between games, that just didn't seem possible. And it wasn't. Kareem was there again, this time with 29 points, 18 of them in the second half when it mattered. The score was tied at 55 at intermission. Kareem had sat much of the second period in foul trouble while Kupchak did admirable work at backup.

The Celtics had played only seven people in the first half, and Magic could see that they were tired. It was written on their faces. Riley told him to keep pushing it at them, not to worry about turnovers. Just keep up the pressure. Keep pushing.

He did.

And the Celtics did something they had never ever done before. They gave up a championship on their home floor, on the hallowed parquet, 111-100. McHale had kept them alive with 36 points, but he got his sixth foul with more than five minutes left. And, thanks in part to Cooper's defense, Bird was closing out a 12-for-29 afternoon. "I thought I'd have a great game today," he said afterward.

In the end, the Lakers' victory was signalled by the squeaking of sneakers in the deathly quiet Garden as the crowd slipped away. It was the same crowd that had so riotously jostled the Lakers the year before.

"We made 'em lose it," Magic said with satisfaction.

Kareem was named the MVP. "He defies logic," Riley said. "He's the most unique and durable athlete of our time, the best you'll ever see. You better enjoy him while he's here."

Magic's ring was sweet redemption, although he had said earlier that he didn't need any. "You wait so long to get back," he admitted afterward. "A whole year. That's the hard part. But that's what makes this game interesting. It's made me stronger. You have to deal with the different situations and see if you can come back."

Magic, certainly, had dealt. And there wasn't anybody watching pro basketball in 1985 who didn't believe that he would deal and deal again.

Camelot in all its glory

The Greatest Team Ever?

Far beyond even what Red Auerbach had ever imagined, Kevin McHale and Robert Parish gave Boston perhaps the most imposing frontcourt in the league. Teamed with Cedric Maxwell, Bird and Scott Wedman in 1984, they could present problems in every facet of the game. As a group, they were brilliant and consistent scorers and superior defenders.

But Maxwell's knee problems changed this special working combination in 1985. Parish and McHale put in extra minutes, and it became obvious that the team needed more depth.

It was particularly obvious to Bill Walton. The former Portland center had traveled basketball's hard road since leading the Trail Blazers to the 1977 NBA title. Foot injuries and foot reconstruction operations had virtually taken him out of the game, leaving his career a frustrating chain of stops and starts. He had left the Trail Blazers in 1978 and eventually dropped out of basketball, opting instead to attend law school at Stanford. He later discovered that he had healed enough to play part-time for the San Diego Clippers. His feet didn't feel too bad in 1985, and he got the notion that perhaps he could help the Celtics, the team that he had always admired. As a backup to Parish, Walton figured he could play just enough to give the team quality center play while Parish or McHale rested. Walton contacted Red Auerbach, who consulted Larry Bird, who thought it was a great idea. Shortly thereafter, the Celtics traded Maxwell to the Clippers for big Bill.

It was the kind of deal that brought immediate scrutiny. Why would the Celtics want to gamble on Walton when every season brought a recurrence of the injuries? The answer became apparent just a matter of games into the 1985-86 schedule—Boston had combined the greatest passing center with the greatest passing forward in the game. The result was an exhibition of ball movement and team play that left the rest of the NBA in another class. In December, they lost a game to Portland in Boston Garden. It would be their only home loss of the year.

At the heart of their performance was a team hunger, almost a craziness.

Guard Jerry Sichting joined the team in the offseason and remembers being amazed at the intensity level when Boston traveled to Los Angeles for a preseason game in October 1985. It was as if the Finals competition had resumed immediately, only stronger. While Kareem Abdul-Jabbar and Walton had both played at UCLA, they held no lost love for each other.

The electric atmosphere in the Forum that night soon transformed into lightning and a fight soon broke out that resulted in a massive on-court pileup.

Sichting remembers the officials untangling the pile to find Boston coach K.C. Jones, rumpled suit and all, at the very bottom.

It was then, Sichting said, that he realized he was about to catch a ride on a whirlwind.

The Celtics roared out on a winning tear that converted doubters at every stop. "Right now, there's no doubt that Boston is a much better team," Magic Johnson said in February 1986 after the Celtics beat the Lakers in the Forum to extend their record to 41-9. On their way to a club-record 67-15 season, the Celtics would claim a winning record against every team in the league.

Few people foresaw this amazing turnaround, including Bird, who had contemplated sitting out the '86 season because of back pain. But the acquisition of Walton and Sichting from Indiana had convinced him it would be wise to hang around and see how things turned out. His reward was the kind of season that only superstars can dream about. He averaged 25.8 points and nearly seven assists, two steals and 10 rebounds per game. He shot .423 from three-point range and finished first in the league in free-throw percentage. For the second consecutive season, Bird broke the 2,000 point mark. And he finished the year with 10 triple doubles.

At the All-Star game in Dallas in February, Bird had 23 points, seven steals, eight rebounds and five assists. Then he won the long-range shootout, and afterward raised his arms in triumph, shouting "I'm the three-point king!"

Later, midway through the NBA Finals, he would pick up his third league MVP award. "I just felt there was no one in the league who could stop me if I was playing hard," Bird said in accepting the award. "What makes me tough to guard is that once I'm near the three point line, I can score from anywhere on the court. It's kind of hard to stop a guy who has unlimited range."

Sampson was tall, but not tall enough.

His personal confidence was at an all-time high, and it infused the team and coursed through the roster. Despite a sore Achilles tendon that forced him to miss 14 games in the middle of the season, McHale responded to his first year as a full-time starter by averaging 21.3 points. His .574 field-goal percentage was fifth best in the league. He blocked 134 shots during the regular season and another 43 during the playoffs. The former two-time Sixth Man award winner was named to the All-Star team and to the NBA All-Defensive first team.

Walton, meanwhile, jumped into McHale's vacancy and claimed the Sixth Man award. He played 80 regular season games for the Celtics (a career high for Walton) and gave them 20 minutes per outing. He shot .562 from the floor and had 162 assists.

The team's other acquisition, Sichting, shot an amazing .570 from the floor as a backcourt sub.

And Parish averaged 9.5 rebounds and 16.1 points per game while shooting .549 from the floor. On occasion, he and Walton played side-by-side in a twin towers setup. The towers became triplets at times when McHale joined them in the lineup. And if K.C. Jones didn't need size, he could go to a smaller, quicker group with Bird, Wedman and McHale. The backcourt had similar depth with Ainge, Dennis Johnson, Sichting, David Thirdkill and Rick Carlisle, all of whom contributed minutes, scoring and defense.

The season took an unexpected turn when Houston eliminated the Lakers in the Western Conference Finals, 4-1. Los Angeles had reshuffled its lineup, releasing Robert McAdoo and Jamaal Wilkes and picking up veteran power forward Maurice Lucas in a trade and rookie A.C. Green through the draft. The Lakers got off to a good start on their way to a 62-20 record, but the chemistry wasn't there in the spring.

The Rockets, on the other hand, played with confidence and enthusiasm. With Bill Fitch as coach, they sported their own twin towers, 7'4" Ralph Sampson at forward and

K.C. was the perfect coach for this veteran team.

6'11" Hakeem Olajuwon at center. Jim Petersen was the backup power forward, while Robert Reid and Rodney McCray worked the other corner. The guards included Mitch Wiggins, Allen Leavell and Lewis Lloyd. John Lucas had played most of the season in the backcourt but fell by the wayside with a springtime recurrence of his drug problem. The Rockets, though, adjusted to this setback and claimed the Midwest Division title with a 51-31 record. They ousted Sacramento and Denver

rather quickly before losing the first game against the Lakers in the Forum, then coming back to sweep four straight. Their fourth victory against Los Angeles came on a buzzer-beating, turnaround jumper by Sampson in the Forum. Houston had set up the final play with a mere second on the clock. Sampson caught the inbounds pass, whirled and released. The ball hit the rim, bounded high, and fell right to the bottom of Laker hearts.

Boston scorched Chicago 3-0,

Walton and Sichting made Boston's bench a force.

Atlanta, 4-1, and Milwaukee, 4-0, in a searing playoff drive, then had to wait eight days for the Finals to begin on Monday May 26. The Celtics were highly favored, and for good reason. For the Rockets to win, Sampson had to play well, which didn't always happen. A solid defensive rebounder with a soft shooting touch and excellent mobility and quickness for a big man, Sampson had been plagued by inconsistency since becoming the top pick in the 1983 draft. He had also been prone to foul trouble at times.

In Game 1, both of those plagues returned. And they weren't pretty. Sampson picked up his third foul just five minutes into the first period. He spent the rest of the half on the bench, and when he did return in the second half, he missed 12 of his first 13 shots. Olajuwon tried to compensate for Sampson's absence with 33 points and 12 rebounds. But McHale and Parish powered around the frontcourt at will, while Bird polished his all-around game with 21 points, 13 assists, eight rebounds and four steals. His double-teaming on Olajuwon helped frustrate the Rockets further.

The Celtics shot 66 percent from the floor for the game. Ainge and Johnson had a big third quarter, and the whole team floated on a high-octane confidence. They won, 112-100, and privately wondered if they weren't headed for another sweep.

That untouchable mentality carried right through Game 2, in which Bird failed to pick up a single foul despite double-teaming Olajuwon much of the game. He did, however, get 31 points, eight rebounds, seven assists, four steals and two blocks. He worked McCray over on offense, backing in to take any of an assortment of shots or working the pick and roll with Parish. Sampson played better and finished with 18 points and eight rebounds. But he still seemed intimidated by Boston Garden. The Celtics ran away with the third quarter, 34-19, and won it, 117-95.

Bird's performance had left Olajuwon awestruck. "He's the greatest player I've ever seen," the Houston center told reporters. Still, Olajuwon said that once the Rockets

got back to Houston for the next three games, he didn't see how the Celtics could beat them in the Summit.

In the time off between venues, Bird received his MVP award. And once in the Summit, he again rang up big numbers—25 points, 15 rebounds, 11 assists and four steals. Running their break smoothly, the Celtics

As expected, the Beantown crowd was ready to ambush Sampson for Game 6.

seemed in control in the third period with a 76-65 lead. But then Fitch switched Robert Reid to cover Bird, and the Boston forward shot three for 12 in the second half. On offense, Sampson found his comfort zone and powered Houston into the lead in the fourth period. He finished with 24 points and 22 rebounds. In the closing minutes, the Rockets ripped through a 9-0 run and took a 103-102 lead with 67 seconds to go. Boston regained the lead when Ainge scored. But Wiggins answered on a tap-in and then the Houston defense forced Boston into a bad shot. Later Parish stepped on the sideline as Boston was inbounding the ball, and Houston survived, 106-104.

"They got lucky," Bird said.

Game 4, of course, was the test. Parish faced down Houston's big men to lead Boston with 22 points and 10 rebounds. Then Bird took over in

prime time. With the score tied at 101 and a little over two minutes left, he threw in a trey. Then on a last-minute Boston possession, Walton rammed home an offensive rebound. Combined, the scores gave the Celtics a 106-103 win and a 3-1 lead in the series.

Game 5, on Thursday June 5, is remembered for a silly fight between Sampson and Sichting. With a little more than three minutes gone in the second period, the Houston forward and Boston's reserve guard got tangled up over the ball. They had words, which led to Sampson throwing punches, one of which struck D.J. in the left eye when he attempted to break things up. Sichting later joked that his sister hit harder than Sampson and that he wasn't sure whether the blow was "a punch or a mosquito bite." But the outburst resulted in Sampson's ejection. Rather than fold, the Rockets found motivation in the incident. They got inspired backup play from Petersen. And Olajuwon put on a grand show with 32 points, 14 rebounds and eight blocks. In the end, the Celtics weren't sure what they had stirred up in Houston, but they knew they didn't want to stir it up again. The Rockets blasted 'em, 111-96, and the series stood at 3-2. Fortunately for the Celtics, it was headed back to Boston Garden, where their combined record for the regular and post season was 49-1.

As expected, the Beantown crowd was ready to ambush Sampson for Game 6. When the Rockets got off their team bus for the shootaround that morning, they were greeted by the jeers of a rowdy gathering. And before game time, Celtics radio announcer Johnny Most roasted Sampson as gutless and yellow, and every time the Houston forward touched the ball, the Garden regulars booed to their hearts' delight. "Sampson Is A Sissy" read one poster. "Sampson you fight like Delilah," read another. The atmosphere made for a tough time for Ralph. He missed his first seven shots before punctuating his frustration with a dunk in the second period. On the day, he would total only eight points.

"I just played bad," a dejected Sampson said later when asked if the crowd had affected him.

Bird, meanwhile, was afire, yelling at his teammates, pushing the action and diving for loose balls. He finished the first half with 16 points, eight rebounds and eight assists to give Boston a 55-38 lead. His teammates knew he wanted the ball. "Just by getting mad and storming around, I got everybody's attention," he said later. "I didn't want this day to slip away from me."

It didn't.

In the third period he sharpened the heart stakes, driving home a flurry of three-point shots. That and Boston's swarming defense sent the Rockets down hard. The Celtics led by 30 in the fourth period and went on to claim their 16th championship, 114-97. On the day, Bird rang up 29 points, 11 rebounds, 12 assists and three steals. The player that Bill Fitch had initiated into the league had disassembled his old coach's new team. Nobody appreciated his performance more than Fitch himself.

"Once the lights go out and play starts, the crowd has more effect on Larry than anyone I've ever seen," the Houston coach said. "I've never seen him more intense than he was today."

(At his retirement, Bird conceded that his emotions had never been higher than before Game 6 in 1986. "I never had a feeling like that before in my life," he said. "My heart was pounding so hard, I thought I was having a heart attack. I loved it [playing at that level], but I never got there again.")

"He is undoubtedly, in my mind at least, the best basketball player playing the game today," Dennis Johnson told reporters afterward. Despite the praise, Bird played the perfectionist. "I've got some things to work on," he said. "I'm not real comfortable with my moves to the basket. By next fall, I want four or five moves I can go to. If I do that, I think I'll be unstoppable."

As a team, Boston had concluded its most impressive season. The Garden parquet had never been more hallowed. Throughout the regular season and the playoffs, the Celtics

Hakeem found little room to operate inside.

had run up a 50-1 homecourt record. The image, of course, was that they had done it with their Bird-led offense. But their defense, in particular, had befuddled the Rockets. "I don't remember the last time I was hounded by a team more than I was today," Sampson said. "Every time I touched the ball, there were two and three guys around me. And that went for Akeem, too."

None of the defense was accidental, K.C. Jones said with pride. "Our defensive intensity was phenomenal. We contested every pass and every dribble. They were under constant pressure every time they touched the ball."

With their third championship, Bird and his Celtics had evened the ring count with Magic and his Lakers. The

balance of the decade was there for the taking, and both sides knew it. The Celtics, though, figured they were developing an edge. Due to the 1984 Gerald Henderson trade with Seattle, Boston had the number two overall pick in the 1986 draft. With it, Red Auerbach planned to select Maryland forward Len Bias. He wasn't another Michael Jordan, but many observers thought he was close. And he would be just the infusion of talent and athleticism to put the Celtics back on top.

THE RUBBER MATCH

Just days after the Lakers' 1986 playoffs loss to Houston, owner Jerry Buss wanted to trade Worthy to Dallas for Mark Aguirre. But Jerry West eventually talked him out of that deal, saying no team wanted to make a trade based on emotions. Bird and his Celtics had held their breath, hoping that Buss would break up the team. But Worthy stayed, and the Lakers went about the business of proving that West's decision was a wise one.

Then their big boost arrived February 13, when the front office acquired Mychal Thompson from San Antonio. Bird was heartsick at the news. How could the Spurs give Thompson to the Lakers? he asked. The 6'10" Thompson could play backup to Kareem at center, and he was a solid power forward. Better yet, he was an excellent low-post defender, and having played with McHale at the University of Minnesota, he knew better than anyone how to defend against Boston's long-armed forward. With Thompson, the Lakers surged to a 65-win regular season, the best in the NBA.

All the while, Boston's fortunes were headed in the other direction.

It had been 18 seasons since a team had won back-to-back championships in the NBA. The 1986-87 Celtics had hopes of being the first modern team to stretch to that achievement. But, one-by-one, things fell apart for them. Tragedy struck the day after the draft when Len Bias, the second player chosen behind Brad Daugherty, collapsed and died from cocaine-induced heart failure. From what investigators could determine, the incident was either the first time, or among the first times, Bias had used the drug. Yet it cost him his life and destroyed the Celtics' future plans. Like that, the second pick of the first round was gone. From there, the team's troubles came in waves.

The Boston bench, which seemed so deep in 1986, rapidly disintegrated. After an early-season accident on a stationary bike, Bill Walton was sidelined with the foot injuries that had plagued him throughout his career. Scott Wedman was struck down by a heel injury and never played for Boston again, and Sichting was slowed by a persistent virus. To bolster the frontcourt, the Celtics picked up Darren Daye and Fred Roberts, but they needed time to build confidence and develop. Without a

Larry pulled the trigger on a trey.

43

Ainge came into his own as an offensive threat.

strong bench, the Boston starters were forced to play Herculean minutes. As a result, Ainge, Bird and Parish were all troubled by nagging injuries. Then, late in the season, Kevin McHale broke a navicular bone in his right foot and tore ligaments as well. The doctors were worried that continued play might cause McHale permanent damage, but because the Celtics seemed to have a good chance in the playoffs, he decided to play hurt.

In time, of course, they would learn that McHale's effort didn't matter. If bad luck hadn't finished off the Celtics, Magic Johnson would find a way to get the job done. They finished the regular schedule at 59-23, the best in the Eastern Conference, but they quickly found themselves in one brutal playoff struggle after another.

Walton had returned in March, but his effort was almost painful to watch. He helped in the first round as Boston eliminated Chicago, 3-0. But after that, he never regained his touch and never performed well enough to contribute. Boston survived Milwaukee in a seven-game Eastern semifinal, then bashed heads with Detroit in the Eastern finals. Again the series went to seven games, and Boston escaped, but only by the virtue of Bird's last-second steal of an Isiah Thomas pass in game

5. Bird quickly fed Dennis Johnson for the winning layup, a play for the ages if there ever was one.

That, however, would just about conclude the Celtics' highlight clips for 1987.

Detroit assistant Dick Versace scouted the Lakers during the playoffs and came away shaking his head. "They're cosmic," he said. "They're playing better than any team I've ever seen."

Denver fell 3-0 in the first round. Then Golden State dropped out of sight, 4-1. Seattle, the opponent in the Western Finals, could only have hoped to do as well. The Sonics went down, 4-0. All of which had been very nice for the Lakers, but they concluded their conference work on May 25, while the Detroit-Boston series was just getting interesting. Faced with a week off, Riley set up a mini camp in Santa Barbara to keep the guys focused.

They had a pancakes-and-strawberries breakfast buffet on Saturday May 30 and watched the Celtics advance with a 117-114 win over Detroit.

Three days later, on Tuesday June 2, the Finals opened in the Forum before a crowd peppered with celebrities. The regulars, Jack Nicholson and Dyan Cannon, were there, but the series would attract oh so many more. Bruce Willis and Don Johnson. Whoopi Goldberg and John McEnroe. Johnny Carson and Henry Winkler.

Riley was faced with two probable scenarios. Either the Celtics would come in game-sharp and take it to the Lakers, or they would come in weary from two straight seven-game battles. The latter very quickly established itself as the operating format for the day. Their tongues dragging, the Celtics could do little more than watch the Lakers run weave drills up and down the floor. "The Celtics looked to me like they were keeping up pretty good," Mychal Thompson quipped later, "just at a different pace."

The Lakers ran 35 fast breaks in the first two quarters and led by 21 at intermission. They settled into a canter thereafter, finally ending it, 126-113.

In Game 2, Boston trailed by seven

Walton worked on the Rockets.

Goldilocks on the boards

in the second quarter, when Michael Cooper pushed the Lakers through a 20-10 outburst, accounting all 20 points himself by either scoring or assisting. When it was over, he had made six of seven trey attempts (a record), and his eight assists tied a Finals' record. And the Celtics had spent another day gasping in pursuit of the Laker break. "One of the Laker girls could've scored a layup on us," said backup center Greg Kite. Actually, the Lakers did quite well without the help of any of their girls. Kareem flicked in 10 of 14 shots for 23 points, while Magic put up nice boxy numbers, 20 assists and 22 points.

It all added up to a 141-122 rout, Boston's sixth straight road loss in the playoffs. The L.A. papers enjoyed these developments thoroughly and took to calling the Celtics "Gang Green."

Before doubt crept too far into Celtic minds, they righted themselves in Game 3. Despite his bad ankle, McHale scored 21 points with 10 rebounds to lead Boston to a 109-103 win. The Lakers, particularly Scott, Worthy and Abdul-Jabbar, had struggled.

"Maybe we were just due for a game like that," Magic said. "I know we won't play that way again."

For a brief moment the pressure was off the Celtics. No longer did they have to worry about the big embarrassment. "We're just too good a team to be swept," Bird said. "This was the most important game of the series for us. If we lost, it might've been tough to get up for Game 4. Now it's going to be easy."

Riley expected the worst in Game 4 and got it. Boston went up by 16 just after the half. Jack Nicholson, who had wormed a seat in the upper press area, spent most of the evening getting choke signs from Boston fans. "There was one guy," Nicholson said. "He was giving me the choke sign so hard, I almost sent for the paramedics. He was wearing a gray sweat shirt, and his face turned almost as gray as his shirt. I couldn't believe it."

Shortly thereafter, relief came to Nicholson and the Lakers. L.A. cut the lead to eight with three and a half

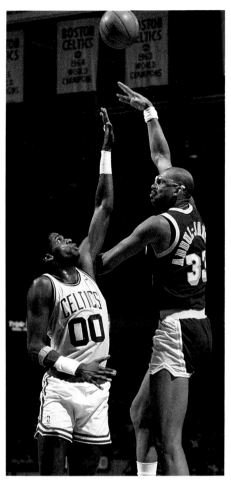

Kareem and Robert

minutes to go in the game. From there, the conclusion, the series actually, came down to one Magic sequence.

With half a minute left, the Lakers took a 104-103 lead and a pick-and-roll to Abdul-Jabbar. But Bird grabbed it back at the 0:12 mark with a three-pointer, putting Boston up 106-104.

On the next possession, Kareem was fouled and went to the line, where he made the first and missed the second. McHale grabbed the rebound, but Mychal Thompson gave him a gentle push and the ball went out of bounds. McHale signalled Boston ball, but the officials pointed the other way.

What followed of course was another of those plays for the ages. For years afterward, Magic Johnson would sit in the private screening room at his mansion, playing and replaying the scene thousands of times, each time tingling with a glee that would refuel his competitive fires. The play replenished his spirit every time he watched it.

Perhaps the definition of a Celtic hell is being assigned to Magic's screening room for eternity, watching the sequence and listening to his delighted laughter over and over and over.

Magic took the ball on the inbounds pass at the left of the key and at first contemplated a 20-footer, but McHale came out to change his mind. So Magic motored into the key, where Bird and Parish joined McHale in a trio of extended arms as Magic lofted a short hook. Parish almost brushed it. But the ball rose up and then descended to a swish. K.C. Jones, watching in a standing twist at the Celtic bench just feet away, felt his heart sink into an abyss.

The Celtics got a timeout with two seconds left, and the Lakers even left Bird open for a shot, which went in. But it didn't stay down, and Magic ran off happily, having stolen Game 4, 107-106.

Red Auerbach, however, was anything but happy. He chased veteran official Earl Strom off the floor, and in front of the press contingency and the television cameras, he made pointed, disparaging remarks, suggesting that Strom was a gelding, that Strom had given the game to the Lakers.

Strom ducked into the officials dressing room, then stuck his head back out to tell Auerbach, "Arnold, you're showing the class that you always have."

Auerbach later explained that he chased Strom in an attempt to fire up his team. "People say, 'Relax, the game is over. The game is over.' Well, the game is never over," he said.

Alas, Red was wrong. The game was most definitely over, and Magic had retired to the locker room to be lost in his eternal joy. He dubbed the shot "my junior, junior, junior sky hook."

"You expect to lose on a sky hook," Bird said with a sickly smile. "You don't expect it to be Magic."

Would the game be remembered just for its last minutes? Bird was asked. "It should," he replied. "A lot happened in the last minute-and-a-half. Robert gets the ball taken away from him. I throw the ball at Kevin's

Celebration '86

feet. They miss a free throw, and we don't get the rebound. How many chances do you need to win a game?"

Before Game 5, Bird told his teammates, "If they want to celebrate, let's not let them do it on the parquet." At one point during the contest, the Laker staff even iced down several cases of champagne. But the Celtics had incentive enough. They got their second win, 123-108, and the series jetted back across the continent.

Kareem arrived for Game 6 with a shave job on his balding head. And for a time, it seemed Los Angeles was intent on cutting it close. Magic had only four points by the half, and the Celtics led, 56-51. But like Kareem's pate, the Lakers glistened after intermission. Worthy finished with 22, and Kareem had 32 points, six rebounds and four blocks. Mychal Thompson had 15 points and nine

rebounds. And Magic led them with another performance of all-around brilliance. On top of his previous efforts, his 16-point, 19-assist, eight-rebound showing brought him the MVP award. And Los Angeles claimed their fourth title of the decade, 106-93.

"Magic is a great, great basketball player," Bird said. "The best I've ever seen."

"He's the best in the game," Riley agreed. "He proved it in the regular season and the playoffs. We wouldn't be anywhere without him. We wouldn't be a championship contender without him."

Magic saw the reflection of his special talents in the team. "This is a super team, the best team I've played on," he said. "It's fast, they can shoot, rebound, we've got inside people, everything. I've never played on a team that had everything before. We've always had to play around

something, but this team has it all."

Bird had to agree. "I guess this is the best team I've ever played against," he said. "In '85, they were good. In '84, I really thought they should have beaten us. . . I don't know if this team's better than they were, but I guess they are. They're fast break is better. They're deeper."

Even with a healthy Bill Walton, the Celtics probably wouldn't have been able to alter the outcome, Bird said. "I would have loved to play them with a Bill Walton and a Scotty Wedman.... We would have given them a hell of a try."

The Lakers and Celtics had established a standard for pro basketball, and by 1987 they had begun to assume that the championship round was theirs to share.

Little did they know that their own private Camelot was slipping away.

Red collects Sweet 16 from the Commissioner.

The Celtics' injury problems would deepen over the ensuing seasons, as would the team's realization of just how big the Bias loss really was.

The years would pass, and Larry and Magic would never again meet in the Finals, with a championship on the line and the world watching.

Yet the spirit of their rivalry would come to rest at the very heart of pro basketball. And the intensity of all future rivalries would be measured against it.

"He was the smartest player I ever played against," Magic said of Bird. "I always enjoyed competing against him because he brought out the best in me. He was the only player that I truly feared."

Larry and Red at the retirement press conference.

The King in his castle.

Reggie has moved into the top echelon.

The Big Three is now Two.

Learning To Fly

The Boston Celtics trailed the New York Knickerbockers in the NBA's Atlantic Division race by five games with just eight games remaining on the schedule in April 1992. Yet the Celtics put together an astounding winning streak, beating Chicago, Cleveland, New York and Detroit twice to win the division title by an eyelash.

There are many treasures in the Celtics' lore, but 1992's miracle finish just may be the most important development in Boston in many seasons.

Down the stretch, with Larry Bird sidelined with back pain, the young Celtics fell in behind Reggie Lewis, Kevin McHale and Robert Parish to win 21 of 22 games.

"We've been staying focused, playing defense and taking care of business," coach Chris Ford observed as he watched the streak unfold.

For years, Boston had been unable to win consistently without Bird's presence on the court. But finally, Ford said, it seemed that this young group of Celtics was learning to play without Larry.

Brown is ready to step up.

And Pinckney stretched to a new level.

Heading into the 1992-93 season, it becomes clear that they learned their lesson none too soon. Just as they were losing Bird to retirement, the young Celtics finally found their wings.

Now the challenge becomes translating that spring finish into a strong fall start.

Second-year forward Rick Fox is unabashed in his belief that it can happen. "At one point, we won 20 out of 21 games," he said during the offseason. "That was a lot of fun, and we were playing well as a team. We closed out the season well, and I believe we can open it up the same way this year.

"Some people say we need another big man, we need this, or we need that. I look to win the championship. The future is now. We still have Robert and Kevin, and we have nothing to lose."

When Bird first injured his back last season, the team seemed lost, Fox said. "But when his back didn't hold up the second time he came back, we decided to go out and get it on our own. A lot of guys, especially Reggie, Kevin and Chief, stepped up."

Looking at this season's roster, there's little reason that the Celtics can't compete, Fox said. "We have a great young backcourt and our frontcourt has a lot of experience."

In fact, the Celtics are deeper than they've been in years. Here's a rundown of how they shape up for 1992-93:

GUARDS

At the point, they have veteran John Bagley, who played a major role in the team's resurgence last spring, plus young talents Dee Brown and Sherman Douglas, who was acquired in a midseason trade for Brian Shaw.

It appears that Brown will again be penciled in as the starter, as he was last season when an early knee injury shortened his season. Brown later rejoined the roster but couldn't take the job away from Bagley, who provided the Celtics with just the spark they needed.

Fox enjoyed a solid rookie season. . .

. . . while Bagley simply saved the show.

Reggie's quiet leadership will be a factor.

"I don't mind it at all," Brown said, of sharing the point guard chores with Bagley in the spring of 1992. "He's playing well. If the flow is going good with me, Doc [Ford] stays with me. And if it's going good with Bags, he stays with him.

"I try to watch [Bagley] as much as I can. It's a blessing watching him. Last year I was watching Brian [Shaw]. But we are both young, and if he'd make a mistake on the court, I'd make it, too.

"You look at Bags, and he's a veteran point guard. You pick up a lot of things from him. I have learned a lot—the penetration, passes, things I had picked up in the summer watching tapes of other point guards."

If that same scenario develops this season, Brown says he will again adjust his approach. Some observers even suggest that Brown is perfectly suited as a third guard, capable of playing both spots. But he doesn't agree.

"For me to be a big contributor to this team and to make an impact in the league, I have to play the one [point] guard," he said in July. "I can play the two guard, but I'm best at the point. I think I have pretty good judgment, I can get the ball up the court, and I play good defense one on one."

The injury, he said, made him aware of how precious his athletic career is. "I was right there before the injury," he added. "I had my skills where I wanted them. I was very comfortable, very relaxed running the team."

Coming back from the injury, Brown was impatient at first. But he observed how off guard Reggie Lewis was capable of making difficult adjustments without putting pressure on himself.

Brown decided he needed to be more like Lewis.

Which is what a lot of NBA players would like to do.

Reggie has simply developed from a shy rookie five seasons ago into one of the best in the game.

"He's one of the top three shooting guards in the league," Brown said, voicing an opinion echoed by the likes of Chuck Daly, Lenny Wilkens and numerous other coaches. "There's

Lewis found a place among the stars.

Michael Jordan and Clyde Drexler, and then you gotta go with Lewis. You got to. On offense, he's unstoppable one on one. And his defense has picked up. He blocks shots, gets steals, and it's one of those things that you can't teach."

If anyone will be called upon to fill Bird's shoes, it will be Lewis. And Brown says the sixth-year guard has some of the qualities that Larry brought to the team.

The big factors are a personal confidence that is infectious to the team and his ability to score when the pressure hits the high side.

"You know you're always in a game with Reggie," Brown said. "It's like when Larry was playing."

Reggie's game begins with his consistently level emotional approach, Brown said. "He never changes expression. Everybody gets mad every once in a while. But

Reggie's always on an even keel whether he scores 40 or he scores four. Because he's always playing hard, he knows what he's got to do.

"It's good to have a backcourt mate who you know you can go to every time, a guy who's gonna hold his own. You can get after yours, and he can take care of his own. It's like Jordan and whoever plays alongside him. Reggie's that type of player now. He's into that caliber."

It seemed that opponents last year were caught off guard by Reggie's rapid development, Brown said. "He snuck up on everybody. Everybody knew he was going to bust onto the scene, but not as much as he did, especially in the playoffs. He stepped it up two or three levels."

Indeed, Lewis jumped from the 20 points per game he was averaging during the regular season to nearly 28 per game in the playoffs.

Reggie says he's ready to take the lead.

Gamble continues to surprise and impress.

It's unclear just how much help the backcourt will get from this year's top rookie, Jon Barry of Georgia Tech, the son of Hall of Famer Rick Barry. He missed rookie camp in a contract dispute and had not signed as training camp neared.

THE X-MAN AND THE FRONTCOURT

However, news in the frontcourt was extremely good for the Celtics, who announced the signing of unrestricted free agent Xavier McDaniel within days after Bird's retirement.

McDaniel had played a major role in the rise of the Knicks to the Eastern Finals in last season's playoffs, and his signing a Boston contract stunned many across the NBA, including New York management.

But McDaniel, who took Bird's open $1.65 million salary slot, said he had long admired Bird and Boston and was eager to go for a league title. His addition also helped the Celtics subtract from New York's growing power.

There were some questions about his knees, but the depth he brings to the Celtics' front line is substantial. McHale and Parish return there for another season, and McDaniel should help spread the minutes around, thus allowing the team to get the best out of what may be the veterans' last season. And power forward Ed Pinckney also is back after a tremendous season last year. Joe Kleine has established himself as an excellent backup center, better than the starters on other teams.

All of which leaves coach Chris Ford reasonably optimistic.

"The Bird Era has come to an end," he said after Bird's announcement. "We'll start building again. We think we have some fine young players. Do we have all the right ingredients? Probably not. But we have time."

The addition of McDaniel has improved that outlook tremendously.

These newer Celtics are learning to fly.

And with a little luck and a good tail wind, they just might sail up the mountain.

Ford ponders the future.

"When they found out about him, they still couldn't do anything about it," Brown said of opponents trying to stop Lewis. "It was one of those things where we were going to him, and they still couldn't do anything.

"It was like when Larry was in his prime."

With Bird's retirement, Lewis has encountered immediate speculation that, like Larry, he will carry the team.

"I'm trying to get my shoulders bigger," he jokingly told Peter May of the *Boston Globe.* "The way I look at it, it's another challenge, and I'm looking forward to it. I feel I'm ready for it. I'm not going to be a different person. I won't be vocal, or tell guys to do this or that. I'm a leader by example. I learned from what Larry did."

The Celtics' guard corps is further bolstered by small forwards Kevin

Gamble and Rick Fox, both of whom can play guard. Gamble, in particular, elevated his play last season as the team's starting small forward. He played well in the playoffs and erased doubts about his defensive desire.

Fox also had a promising rookie season. "He proved he belongs," said Celtics president Red Auerbach.

Fox credits his college experience at the University of North Carolina under Dean Smith as one of the factors in his relatively easy adjustment to Boston's tradition. "I had a great teacher in college, someone who instilled in me the basics and the confidence to compete at this level," Fox said. "For me to move into a franchise that teaches team play makes it all the easier."

The season wasn't without low spots for the rookie, but he found a level of consistency and adjusted.

The Chief seems ageless.

Carded

Seniority Plus

I t seems to be one of those good stories that just keeps getting better.

Robert Parish, at 39, is the oldest player in the NBA. And still very much of a factor in every Celtics game. The numbers alone defy belief.

Including playoffs, he has played in 1,434 games for a total of 44,669 minutes, 23,379 points, and 14,405 rebounds.

Just about all the territory ahead of him is uncharted except for the swath cut by Kareem Abdul-Jabbar, who retired in 1989 at age 42.

Parish said he hasn't consulted with Kareem about career planning, but he has contemplated what kept the great Los Angeles center going.

"I definitely know what the motivating factor was besides the opportunity to play with Magic," the Chief said. "It was the opponents, because every center he played against was younger than he was. And they used him as a measuring stick because he was a legendary center."

That same scenario keeps Parish striding to center court for the opening tip game after game. He is not, however, motivated by increasing the measure of his own legend. "Maybe when I retire I'll look back on it in those terms," he said. "But right now I really don't think about it."

Neither does he have a particular calendar for his own career. "I'll take it one year at a time," he said. "I have another year to fulfill on my contract, and after that, we'll see what happens."

The conditioning is impeccable

The countenance regal

Leprechaun redux

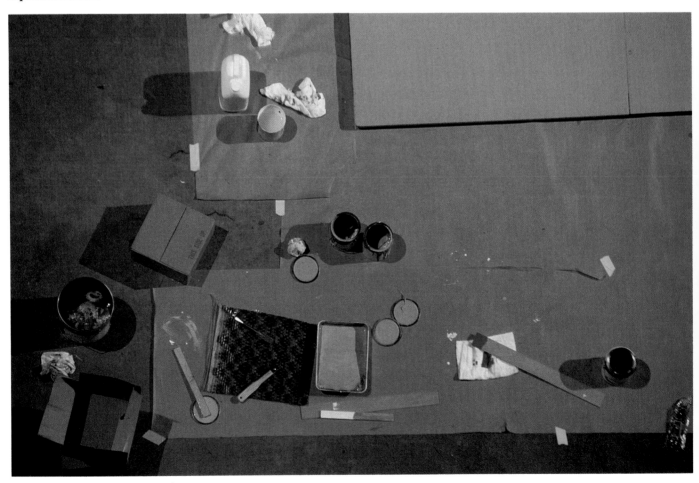

Green, again, is the dominant color.

66

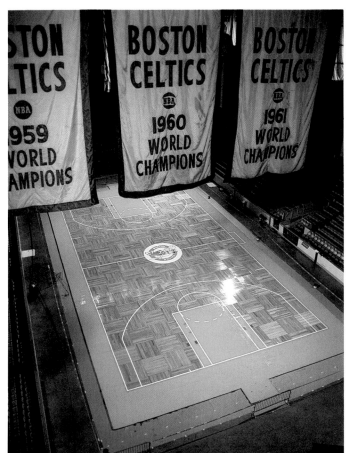

Garden, stripped

And finished

The Parquet Gets A Facelift

The famed parquet floor in Boston Garden has a long history.

It actually first appeared in Boston Arena shortly after World War II. Because of the post-war lumber shortage, the floor was constructed of scrap wood. Thus the parquet design.

The sections were moved to Boston Garden in 1952, which in the ensuing years has served as home to 16 world championship teams.

The current floor in the Garden is actually the third edition but had not been refinished since the early 1970s.

The Garden's employees remedied that in August 1992 with a refinishing that took about two weeks. Now its mirror surface reflects those championship banners in the rafters.

The pieces together

67

Bill Russell works against the Cincinnati Royals. (Photos by Jerry Budley)

Celtics
Flashbacks

Bill Russell

Many of basketball's greatest players have been prolific scorers or flashy ballhandlers. Bill Russell was neither. He was simply the most successful athlete in the history of the game. He led the University of San Francisco to two NCAA championships in 1955 and '56, then helped the U.S. team to the gold medal in the 1956 Olympics in Australia. From there, he ran through an unparalleled professional career as the heart of a Boston Celtics team that won 11 NBA titles in 13 seasons.

Not a bad run for a guy who struggled to get playing time on his high school team.

It seems that even the greatest players have a knock, and the one against Russell was that he couldn't shoot. And, frankly, he wasn't a great passer, either. He scored adequately enough, but he came along in the 1950s when the basketball ideal was a deadeye swisher. The jump shot was coming into vogue, and coaches everywhere seemed infatuated by acrobatic gunners. Russell, on the other hand, was the first of a new breed, the athletic big man. (At 6'9" he could run the 440-yard dash in 49 seconds.) His shot-blocking skills were revolutionary, and his rebounding abilities controlled any game he played in. But far more important, he had a heart and a will dedicated solely to winning.

As Bob Cousy, his former Celtics teammate, once said, "Bill Russell was the ultimate team player."

Russell, Cousy explained, was willing to forego the ego thrill of scoring to concentrate on the defense and rebounding that made his team successful.

"I think he's the greatest player to ever put on a uniform," agreed Celtics teammate Sam Jones. "He came to play every night. He gave 100 percent

all of the time. He wanted to WIN."

Russell hated practice, Cousy said. "But once the whistle blew, no one matched his intensity. There hasn't been a center to come along since to do the things he did in rebounding and shotblocking."

Russell was raised and schooled amid the ugliness of segregation, and the constant insult of 1950s racism seemed to drive him, Cousy said. "I think it had a lot to do with his basic anger at the world. A lot of it was 'whitey,' and he was going to get 'whitey.' Russ, to this day, is the angry man."

Considering his background, Russell's lack of offensive polish wasn't surprising. He recalled in his autobiography, *Second Wind*, that he was a troubled adolescent desperate for a reason to be positive about himself. As a sophomore at McClymonds High in east Oakland, California, he tried out for the football team but quit after one practice because he thought the coach was abusive. From there, he tried out for the cheerleading squad, but he failed to make the cut. His consolation, he thought, would be junior varsity basketball, but again he was cut. Strangely, though, the school's varsity coach encouraged him to come out for that team. It seemed crazy, to make the varsity after being cut from the jayvees. But the coach, George Powles, convinced him it was worth a try.

In basketball, Russell found something he could turn his energies to. Still, it wasn't an automatic thing. Although a bit awkward, he could run and jump quite well, but he froze with fear any time the ball came near him. Later, when he made an infrequent appearance as a varsity substitute, students from his own school hooted at him. That, in turn, drove him to work harder, and by the latter part of his senior season, he had begun to make substantial progress, only by

then it was too late for college scouts to take notice.

He had, however, caught the attention of Hal DeJulio, an alumnus of the University of San Francisco, who asked coach Phil Woolpert to give him a tryout. The coach agreed, and after taking a look at Russell, offered a scholarship. The coach wasn't completely sold on the big youngster, but Russell had height and a degree of agility.

At San Francisco, Russell met lifelong friend and teammate K.C. Jones. Russell found that Jones, like himself, believed in defense almost out of desperation. Woolpert, too, was a defensive fanatic, and the three of them put together one of the most fearsome defensive units in the history of college basketball.

After leading his team to two national titles at San Francisco, Russell joined the Celtics and resumed his championship drive.

Russell went on to lead Boston to 11 NBA titles before he retired in 1969. In 1991, he still owned just about every major NBA Finals rebounding record. He pulled down 19 boards in one quarter during the 1962 Finals against the Lakers. And twice—in 1960 against St. Louis and 1962 against Los Angeles—he had 40 rebounds in an NBA Finals game.

Russell outdueled Wilt Chamberlain, the primary adversary of his career, in just about every major meeting, a fact that has left many fans speculating how he would have done against other great centers from other eras. Computer analysis once suggested that Kareem Abdul-Jabbar (Lew Alcindor) might have gotten the best of Russell.

Red Auerbach, of course, disagreed.

"Computers can never creep into people's competitive attitudes," Auerbach said. "Not that Abdul-Jabbar wasn't a great competitor. But Russell

Russell, as player and coach

continually rose to occasions. Abdul-Jabbar did, too. Abdul-Jabbar was a giant among men. He was so much bigger than everybody else. What would have happened if they were playing face-to-face? I don't know. Russell would have done something to affect Kareem's sky hook. Look at how Russell adjusted against Chamberlain. To me, he outplayed Chamberlain nine out of 10 times."

No one can answer such a question, Cousy said. "But if Jabbar had had Russell's intensity, it wouldn't be close."

Those who played with and against Russell have little doubt that he is the greatest player ever. Asked how Big Bill would fare in the modern NBA game, Hall of Famer Tom Gola was quick with an answer. "Nobody," he said, "could touch Russell."

Sharman in action

Bill Sharman

His friends called him Willie. It was a term of endearment but it didn't begin to indicate Bill Sharman's toughness. His reputation today is that of one of the game's great early shooters. That, too, is misleading. Shooters are considered specialists, guys who languish on the perimeter where they take the open shots while everybody else mixes it up. In other words, shooters play soft.

There was never anything soft about Sharman's game.

He was rare, because not only was he a great shooter, but he was a tenacious defensive player as well. Bob Cousy said he always figured he had the most intense killer instinct in basketball—until he met Sharman.

"Bill matched mine," Cousy admitted.

Sharman wasn't known for excessive fighting. But when he did square off, whether the opponent was a seven-footer or just another guard, the bouts were usually one-punch affairs.

"Willie didn't talk," Ed Macauley recalled. "When he'd had enough, you knew it."

His one-punch victims included 6'9", 230-pound Nobel Jorgensen of the Syracuse Nationals and Hall of Famer Andy Phillip.

Sharman's skill at pugilism, though, was no greater than any of his other athletic abilities. He was good at everything he did. He lettered in five sports (football, basketball, baseball, tennis and track) in high school in Porterville, California. After retirement from pro basketball, he became a scratch golfer.

"He's the best athlete I've ever been around," Cousy said, which is no small statement considering Cousy's substantial playing, coaching and broadcasting career.

After a stint in the Navy during World War II, Sharman played basketball at Southern Cal, where he was a 6'2" forward in a controlled offense, a background that didn't exactly prepare him for prominence in pro basketball. He gave pro baseball a try with the Brooklyn Dodgers organization before coming to the NBA with the Washington Capitols for 1951.

Auerbach picked him up after Washington folded, a development that allowed Sharman to prosper. Having been a forward in college, he wasn't a good ballhandler. In Boston, he played alongside Cousy, which allowed him to focus on his shooting and defense.

The Celtics ran a freewheeling system. Auerbach was unique among coaches in that he understood what it took to win, Cousy said. When you have talented players, you allow them to play. The Celtics of the 1950s had six basic plays and three variations of each of those for about 16 different options. But they relied on the freelance and transition situations as often as possible because they played best that way.

"Sharman was just perfect for it because he moved constantly," Cousy said. Other players around the league hated to defend him because he ran continuously.

"He would move in a circle, and eventually he would come free," Cousy said. "I almost knew where he was going before he got there." Most often he would circle and emerge on the weak side just as the defense was collapsing, which left him with an open shot. He was a quick shooter, hoisting the ball from his shoulders up.

"He was a complete technician in terms of the mechanics of the shot," Cousy said. "He never took a low percentage shot."

Those mechanics served him at the free throw line as well. For eight seasons he led the league in free-throw percentage. And for four seasons, 1956-59, he led the Celtics in scoring. He relinquished that role to Heinsohn in 1960 and '61, although Sharman continued to average better than 15 points a game.

But with each succeeding season, Sam Jones had become a bigger factor coming off the bench. And by 1961, Sharman was 35 and had played 11 seasons. The opportunity became available for him to coach the Los Angeles franchise in the new American Basketball Association. Sharman knew it made good sense to retire. It was a difficult decision.

"I didn't want to feel I was just hanging on to receive a paycheck," he said.

"He had a lot of pride, and great players are reluctant to stay too long," Auerbach said.

Sharman turned to coaching after his playing days and soon showed that he was among the best. He directed the Utah Stars to the 1971 American Basketball Association championship, and the next season the Los Angeles Lakers hired him to try to end their misery.

They had lost seven straight times in the NBA Finals and desperately wanted to claim a title before Wilt Chamberlain and Jerry West ended their playing careers.

Sharman gave them a unique mix of fight and quiet innovation, all in the same package. He was a Southern California boy, but he was also a Celtic. The Lakers weren't quite sure what to make of him.

"It was difficult for us to relate to him in the beginning, because he was covered with Boston green," recalled Pat Riley, a Laker sub at the time. "But in time we came around. He was a low-key guy, but very competitive, very feisty."

It didn't help that Sharman gave the Lakers another dose of green when he added K.C. Jones as his assistant coach. But the two former Boston guards brought just the right mindset to Los Angeles.

The 1971-72 Lakers won more

games than any team in NBA history with a 69-13 record, which in turn gave them the best winning percentage ever, .841. They had the most ever victories in which they scored over 100 points, 81, the most wins on the road, 31, and the most at home, 38.

Best of all, they rolled off a 33-game win streak, which ended when they lost a road game to rival Milwaukee, 120-114.

"We knew it had to end sometime," Sharman said after the loss. "It was one of our weakest games in quite a while, but I think we learned something from it. It's hard to learn when you win."

With each win, the mounting streak had boosted their team confidence. And when it was over, they knew they had accomplished something.

"We had been so snake-bitten in the '60s, to never ever win, always getting beat by Boston," Riley said. "When we won 33 games in a row, it was incredible."

That spring, the Lakers beat the New York Knicks for the league championship, putting a wrap on the most successful season in NBA history.

Sharman, of course, was the catalyst for it all.

He remained coach for several more seasons, then moved into the general managership of the Lakers and presided over their rise to prominence in the 1980s. He suffered voice damage several years ago and stepped down from his position to make room for West. However Sharman, a Hall of Famer, remains affiliated with the club today as a consultant.

Which leaves only one question.

What is he in his heart of hearts?

Celtic green or Laker blue?

Sharman, the coach

CELTICS

PROFILES

JOHN BAGLEY   54

Position: Guard
Birthplace: Bridgeport, CT
High School: Warren Harding High (CT)
College: Boston College '83
Height: 6-0
Weight: 192
NBA Experience: 10 Years

HOW ACQUIRED: Traded by New Jersey to Boston for 1991 and 1993 second-round draft choices on October 5, 1989.

1991-92 SEASON: Tabbed as Boston's starting point guard due to early season injuries to Dee Brown and Brian Shaw... started the first 22 games and 53 of the first 56; did not start on 12/18, 1/4 and 1/6 (played, but as a reserve)... other starts were 3/17, and 5 games from 4/10-4/19... missed 3 games with injuries: 12/18 (bruised left knee), 1/4 (sprained right ankle) and 3/18 vs. Cleveland (sore right foot); in each instance, the injury was suffered the night before... made all 8 free throws vs. Indiana on 11/20... grabbed his all-time Celtics high of 8 rebounds in 21 minutes at New Jersey on 11/23... tallied 8 consecutive points on 11/29 vs. the Lakers... compiled 65 assists in 7 games from 1/10-1/22, including 4 games of 10 or more... DNP-CD in 6 straight games from 2/28-3/10 when Chris Ford decided to use a tandem of Dee Brown and Sherman Douglas... in 33 minutes vs. Portland on 3/15, totalled 10 assists and 9 points; had 5 points in the second overtime... was tremendous in a win at Detroit that lifted Boston into first place on 4/15; hit a backbreaking 3-point field goal with 51.9 seconds remaining to cap off a season high 18 point, 9 assist, 7 rebound evening... in the season's last 5 games as a replacement for Brown, he contributed 56 assists and 57 points... 10+ minutes 70 times... 20+ minutes 53 times... 30+ minutes 16 times... 40+ minutes once... 10+ points 22 times... 10+ assists 17 times... 10 double-doubles... DNP-CD 6 times... **1992 Playoffs:** Played in more games (10) in 1992 then in his previous nine years combined... had a massive effort in Game 2 vs. Indiana with 35 points and 15 assists; also connected on a rare four-point play... vs. Indiana, he had 35 of Boston's 75 assists and was Boston's second leading scorer with 61 points (20-40, 1-2, 20-28)... 10+ minutes 10 times... 20+ minutes 9 times... 30+ minutes 6 times...

40+ minutes once... 10+ assists 3 times... 10+ points 4 times... 20+ points once... 30+ points once... 3 double-doubles.

PROFESSIONAL CAREER: Drafted by Cleveland on the first-round of the 1982 draft as an undergraduate, the 12th pick overall... in his third NBA season, he accomplished a career best 35 points on February 4, 1985... finished fourth among assists leaders in 1985-86, averaging a team record 9.4 per game... traded by Cleveland (with Keith Lee) to New Jersey for Darryl Dawkins and James Bailey on October 8, 1987... in only five seasons with Cleveland, he became their all-time assists leader with 2,311... passed the 5,000 career scoring mark in 1988-89 and surpassed the 3,000 career assists total in the same season... registered his lone double-double of his first Celtics' season on opening night... started 17 times in 1989-90; season was abbreviated due to a separated left shoulder in November, and a right hamstring strain in February... underwent successful arthroscopic surgery on his right knee in Cleveland on 3/14/91... the surgery found a cartilage fracture of the bone in his right knee and the repair was performed successfully... spent the entire 1990-91 regular season on the injured list.

COLLEGE CAREER: Passed up his final year of eligibility to enter the NBA draft... a three-year starter at Boston College, he led the team in scoring each season... finished fourth on the all-time BC scoring list... named Big East Player of the Year for the 1980-81 campaign... set Big East records for most points (30) and most free throws (16) in one game (January 16, 1981 vs. Villanova)... points per game increased in each season, career average was 17.9.

PERSONAL: John Edward Bagley is single... is one of eight children... founded the Bagley-Walden Foundation with the purpose of helping young people develop strategies for success through the utilization of athletic and academic programs... likes playing tennis... would like to get involved in coaching upon the conclusion of playing career... majored in Sociology... shoe size is 12.

CAREER HIGHS: 35 points at Washington (2-4-85)
11 rebs at Boston (2-6-85)
19 assists at Dallas (3-16-85)

TOP REGULAR SEASON PERFORMANCES (WITH CELTICS)

Points	Rebounds	Assists
18 vs. Indiana (11-20-91)	8 at New Jersey (11-23-91)	16 vs. Milwaukee (11-3-89)
18 at Detroit (4-15-92)	7 at Detroit (4-15-92)	14 at Philadelphia (4-14-92)
14 vs. Phila at Htfd (11-14-89)	7 at New York (12-14-91)	14 at Chicago (4-17-90)
14 vs. LA Lakers (11-29-91)	7 at Milwaukee (3-17-92)	13 two times
14 vs. Miami (4-19-92)		

NBA CAREER RECORD

Year	Team	G	Min	FGM	FGA	Pct.	FTM	FTA	Pct	Off	Def	Tot	Ast	PF-Dq	St	Bl	Pts	Avg
82-83	Clev.	68	990	161	373	.432	64	84	.762	17	79	96	167	74-0	54	5	386	5.7
83-84	Clev.	76	1712	257	607	.423	157	198	.793	49	107	156	333	113-1	78	4	673	8.9
84-85	Clev.	81	2401	338	693	.488	125	167	.749	54	237	291	697	132-0	129	5	804	9.9
85-86	Clev.	78	2472	366	865	.423	170	215	.791	76	199	275	735	165-1	122	10	911	11.7
86-87	Clev.	72	2182	312	732	.426	113	136	.831	55	197	252	379	114-0	91	7	768	10.7
87-88	N.J.	82	2774	393	896	.439	148	180	.822	61	196	257	479	162-0	110	10	981	12.0
88-89	N.J.	68	1642	200	481	.416	89	123	.724	36	108	144	391	117-0	72	5	500	7.4
89-90	Bos.	54	1095	100	218	.459	29	39	.744	26	63	89	296	77-0	40	4	230	4.3
90-91	Bos.			INJURED														
91-92	Bos.	73	1742	223	506	.441	68	95	.716	38	123	161	480	123-1	57	4	524	7.2
TOTALS:		652	17010	2350	5371	.438	963	1237	.778	412	1309	1721	3957	1077-3	753	54	5777	8.9

Three-Point Field Goals:1982-83, 0-for-14; 1983-84, 2-for-17 (.118); 1984-85, 3-for-26 (.115); 1985-86, 9-for-37 (.243); 1986-87, 31-for-103 (.301); 1987-88, 47-for-161 (.292); 1988-89, 11-for-54 (.204); 1989-90, 1-for-18 (.056); 1991-92, 10-for-42 (.238). Totals: 124-for-514 (.241).

PLAYOFF RECORD

84-85	Clev.	4	168	22	56	.393	7	10	.700	1	15	16	40	7-0	10	0	51	12.8
89-90	Bos.	5	70	8	15	.533	3	4	.750	3	1	4	17	9-0	4	1	19	3.8
90-91	Bos.			INJURED														
91-92	Bos.	10	308	42	95	.442	26	37	.703	8	19	27	85	17-0	9	1	111	11.1
TOTALS:		19	546	72	166	.434	36	51	.706	12	35	47	142	33-0	23	2	181	9.5

Three-Point Field Goals:1984-85, 0-for-3; 1989-90, 0-for-1 (.000); 1990-91, 0-for-0 (.000); 1991-92, 1-for-4 (.250).Totals: 1-for-8 (.125).

SEASON/CAREER HIGHS

	FGM	FGA	FTM	FTA	REB	AST	ST	BL	PTS
1991-92/Regular Season	8/16	18/21	8/10	8/12	8/11	14/19	3/6	1/2	18/35
1992/Playoffs	11/11	21/21	12/12	12/12	7/7	15/15	2/6	1/1	35/35

LARRY BIRD 33

Position: Forward
Birthdate: December 7, 1956
Birthplace: West Baden, IN
High School: Springs Valley (French Lick, IN)
College: Indiana State '79
Height: 6-9
Weight: 220
NBA Experience: 13 Years

HOW ACQUIRED: Celtics first-round draft choice in 1978... 6th pick overall.

1991-92 SEASON: A deterrent back injury kept him out of 37 games (team went 20-17)... at Washington on 11/2, he logged team highs in minutes (47), points (31) and rebounds (14); he added 7 assists, and he buried a 3-point field goal with 20.2 seconds left in regulation to give Boston a 112-110 lead... became the NBA's twelfth all-time scorer, as he surpassed Walt Bellamy on 11/5... started the first 20 games before he missed the New York game on 12/14 due to a back ailment; he's missed 7 of the past 10 regular season games played at the Knicks... played in the next 8 games, through the end of December... snatched 36 rebounds in two consecutive games on 12/28-12/30... missed the entire months of January (placed on the injured list on 1/6 due to a sore back) and February before returning on March 1 vs. Dallas... in that game against the Mavericks, he nearly amassed a triple-double with 26 points (9-16, 1-4, 7-7), 13 rebounds and 9 assists... from March 1 to the rest of the season, he played 17 games, 627 (36.9) minutes, 323 (19.0) points (123-267, 21-55, 56-60), 166 (9.8) rebounds, 132 (7.8) assists... made 36 straight free throws before missing on 3/13 vs. New Jersey... in that same contest, moved into the eleventh spot on the NBA's all-time scoring list, surpassing Hal Greer... played 54 minutes vs. Portland on 3/15, recorded 49 points (19-35, 2-8, 9-10), 14 rebounds, 12 assists and 4 steals; had 16 fourth quarter points and made a 3-point field goal with 2 seconds left in regulation to tie the game... in 9 games from 3/4-3/18, he grabbed 79 rebounds of which 78 came off the defensive glass... scored the first 5 points of an 11-0 Boston overtime run at Detroit on 3/20... his last action of the season was on 4/3 in Indiana... 10+ minutes 45 times... 20+ minutes 45 times... 30+ minutes 38 times... 40+ minutes 17 times... 50+ minutes once... 10+ points 42 times... 20+ points 24 times... 30+ points 5 times... 40+ points once... 10+ rebounds 22 times... 10+ assists 4 times... 23 double-doubles... 1 triple-double... finished 8th among league leaders in 3-point field goal percentage and ranked second in free throw percentage. **1992 Playoffs:** Missed the entire Indiana series and the first three games of the Cleveland series due to back pain... in Game 7 at Cavs, he played 33 minutes, and tallied 12 points (6-9 fgs), 5 rebounds and 4 assists... 37 minutes in Game 6 vs. Cavs, his first start since April 3: 16 points (8-18, 0-3, 0-1), 6 rebounds, and a game high 14 assists... 20 minutes in Game 5 at Cavs, 13 points (6-10, 0-1, 1-1), 5 rebounds... in his first action since April 3, he played 17 minutes in Game 4 vs. Cavs, and tallied 4 points (1-5, 0-1, 2-2), 2 rebounds, and 3 assists... 10+ minutes 4 times... 20+ minutes 3 times... 30+ minutes 2 times... 10+ points 3 times... 10+ assists once... 1 double-double.

PROFESSIONAL CAREER: Drafted by Boston on the first-round of the 1978 draft, as a junior eligible, the 6th pick overall... voted the NBA Rookie of the Year in 1980 and was a member of the league's All-Rookie Team... a member of the All-NBA First Team his first nine years, and to the Second Team in his 11th... named to the all-star team 12 times... named the all-star game MVP in 1982... All-Defensive Second Team in 1982, 1983, and 1984... playoff MVP in 1984 and 1986... regular season MVP in 1984, 1985, and 1986; one of only three players in NBA history to achieve

the feat in three consecutive seasons... Player of the Week 15 times... Player of the Month 7 times... NBA ft% leader in 1984, 1986, 1987, and 1990... Boston has never had a r/s losing month with him in the line-up... whenever he plays 3,000 minutes, Boston advances to the NBA Finals; whenever he doesn't, Boston does not advance... only Celtic to score 2,000+ points in three consecutive seasons... 69 triple-doubles, including 59 in the r/s... 40+ points 52 times, 46 in the r/s... 50+ pts 4 times, all in the r/s... was held scoreless on 1/3/81 at Golden State... grabbed 21 rebounds in Game One of the 1981 NBA Finals vs. Houston; his sensational left-handed flying followup of his missed 22-footer came in the middle of the 4th quarter (Boston then trailed 87-86, then won 98-95)... Bird-Erving fight, 11/9/84... set NBA playoff record for most points in one year, 1984... tallied 34 points in Game Five win over the Lakers in the 1984 Finals, despite 97 degree temperatures inside Boston Garden... scored 10,000th career point on 1/11/85 vs. Washington... consecutive game-winning buzzer beaters on 1/27/85 (Portland) and 1/29/85 (Detroit)... set team mark with 60 pts on 3/12/85... named AP Male Athlete of the Year for 1986... named The Sporting News Man of the Year for 1986... won the long distance shootout in the first three years of its existence... triple-double in 1986 title clincher vs. Houston... consecutive 40+ point games on 3/20/87 (Seattle) and 3/22/87 (New Jersey)... achieved a triple-double at halftime on 4/1/87 vs. Washington... on 5/23/87, was ejected with Bill Laimbeer for fighting... made miraculous steal of Isiah Thomas' inbounds pass with five seconds left to give Boston a win in Game Five of their 1987 playoff series... on 11/7/87 at Washington, game-tying 3-pt fg with 4 seconds left in 4th; hit game-winner with no time left in OT... on 11/11/87, he registered Boston's first 40/20 game (42 points and 20 rebs) vs. Indiana... on 5/22/88, in 7th game win vs. Hawks, scored 34 pts including 20 (9-10 fgs) in the 4th... first player in NBA history to register 50% fgs and 90% fts in the same season, and he is the only player to do it twice... missed all but six games in the 1988-89 season due to surgical removal of bone spurs in both heels... had the second best (Calvin Murphy, 78) free throw streak in NBA annals snapped at 71 on 2/13/90 in Houston... achieved his 5,000th career assist on 11/14/90 vs. Charlotte, and became the 15th player to total 20,000 points on 11/30/90 vs. Washington; became the 5th NBA player to reach both those numbers (Jabbar, Robertson, West and Havlicek)... in Game Five clincher vs. Indiana on 5/5/91, he made a Superman-like return after a serious fall to the floor earlier in the game; had a game high 32 points and sparked a game 39-25 run... had 6/7/91 back surgery for a ruptured L4-5; he had congenital stenosis of the foramen where the L5 nerve root exited and he had a problem with rotational and transational instability of the spine - the two hour surgery included the removal of the disc, large fragment which was teased from a bed of scar, and the nerve root was freed out.

COLLEGE CAREER: Consensus All-America in 1978 and 1979 and The Sporting News Player of the Year in 1979... TSN All-America First Team in 1978 and 1979... graduated as the fifth all-time leading NCAA scorer (30.3 ppg)... ISU compiled a record of 81-13 overall and 50-1 at home in his three years... led ISU to the 1979 NCAA Finals... John Wooden Award winner in 1979... also attended Indiana University, and Northwood Institute, but did not play.

PERSONAL: Larry Joe Bird is married to the former Dinah Mattingly; the couple adopted a baby boy, Connor, in 1991... has four brothers and one sister, mother's name is Georgia... avid outdoorsman... likes Kenny Rogers' music... major fan of the St. Louis Cardinals... returns to Indiana during the summer... owns "Larry Bird's Boston Connection," a hotel/restaurant in Terre Haute... on 8/2/84, a street in Terre Haute was named in his honor... holds the annual "Larry Bird Pro All-Star Scholarship Classic" during the off-season in Indiana... shoe size is 13 and a half.

TOP REGULAR SEASON PERFORMANCES

Points
60 vs. Atl. at N.O. (3-12-85)
53 vs. Indiana (3-30-83)
50 at Dallas (3-10-86)
50 vs. Atlanta (11-10-89)
49 vs. Washington (1-27-88)
49 at Phoenix (2-15-88)
49 vs. Portland (3-15-92)

Rebounds
21 at Washington (3-16-82)
21 at Denver (12-29-81)
21 at LA Lakers (2-11-81)
21 at Philadelphia (11-1-80)
20 six times

Assists
17 at Golden State (2-16-84)
16 vs. Cleveland (3-21-90)
15 vs. Washington (4-1-87)
15 vs. Cleveland (3-27-85)
15 vs. Atlanta (1-13-82)
15 vs. Cleveland (11-2-90)

NBA RECORD

Year	Team	G	Min	FGM	FGA	Pct	FTM	FTA	Pct	Off	Def	Tot	Ast	PF-Dq	St	Bl	Pts	Avg
79-80	Bos.	82	2955	693	1463	.474	301	360	.836	216	636	852	370	279-4	143	53	1745	21.3
80-81	Bos.	82	3239	719	1503	.478	283	328	.863	191	704	895	451	239-2	161	63	1741	21.2
81-82	Bos.	77	2923	711	1414	.503	328	380	.863	200	637	837	447	244-0	143	66	1761	22.9
82-83	Bos.	79	2982	747	1481	.504	351	418	.840	193	677	870	458	197-0	148	71	1867	23.6
83-84	Bos.	79	3028	758	1542	.492	374	421	.888	181	615	796	520	197-0	144	69	1908	24.2
84-85	Bos.	80	3161	918	1760	.522	403	457	.882	164	678	842	531	208-0	129	98	2295	28.7
85-86	Bos.	82	3113	796	1606	.496	441	492	.896	190	615	805	557	182-0	166	51	2115	25.8
86-87	Bos.	74	3005	786	1497	.525	414	455	.910	124	558	682	566	185-3	135	70	2076	28.1
87-88	Bos.	76	2965	881	1672	.527	415	453	.916	108	595	703	467	157-0	125	57	2275	29.9
88-89	Bos.	6	189	49	104	.471	18	19	.947	1	36	37	29	18-0	6	5	116	19.3
89-90	Bos.	75	2944	718	1517	.473	319	343	.930	90	622	712	562	173-2	106	61	1820	24.3
90-91	Bos.	60	2277	462	1017	.454	163	183	.891	53	456	509	431	118-0	108	58	1164	19.4
91-92	Bos.	45	1662	353	758	.466	150	162	.926	46	388	434	306	82-0	42	33	908	20.2
TOTALS:		897	34443	8591	17334	.496	3960	4471	.886	1757	7217	8974	5695	2279-11	1556	755	21791	24.3

Three-Point Field Goals: 1979-80, 58-for-143 (.406); 1980-81, 20-for-74 (.270); 1981-82, 11-for-52 (.212); 1982-83, 22-for-77 (.286); 1983-84, 18-for-73 (.247); 1984-85, 56-for-131 (.427); 1985-86, 82-for-194 (.423); 1986-87, 90-for-225 (.400); 1987-88, 98-for-237 (.414); 1988-89, 0-for-0 (.000); 1989-90, 65-for-195 (.333); 1990-91, 77-for-198 (.389); 1991-92, 52-for-128 (.406); Totals: 649-for-1727 (.376).

PLAYOFF RECORD

Year	Team	G	Min	FGM	FGA	Pct	FTM	FTA	Pct	Off	Def	Tot	Ast	PF-Dq	St	Bl	Pts	Avg
79-80	Bos.	9	372	83	177	.469	22	25	.880	22	79	101	42	30-0	14	8	192	21.3
80-81	Bos.	17	750	147	313	.470	76	85	.894	49	189	238	103	53-0	39	17	373	21.9
81-82	Bos.	12	490	88	206	.427	37	45	.822	33	117	150	67	43-0	23	17	214	17.8
82-83	Bos.	6	240	49	116	.422	24	29	.828	20	55	75	41	15-0	13	3	123	20.5
83-84	Bos.	23	961	229	437	.524	167	190	.879	62	190	252	136	71-0	54	27	632	27.5
84-85	Bos.	20	815	196	425	.461	121	136	.890	53	129	182	115	54-0	34	19	520	26.0
85-86	Bos.	18	770	171	331	.517	101	109	.927	34	134	168	148	55-0	37	11	466	25.9
86-87	Bos.	23	1015	216	454	.476	176	193	.912	41	190	231	165	55-1	27	19	622	27.0
87-88	Bos.	17	763	152	338	.450	101	113	.894	29	121	150	115	45-0	36	14	417	24.5
88-89	Bos.	0	0	0	0	.000	0	0	.000	0	0	0	0	0-0	0	0	0	0.0
89-90	Bos.	5	207	44	99	.444	29	32	.906	7	39	46	44	10-0	5	5	122	24.4
90-91	Bos.	10	396	62	152	.408	44	51	.863	8	64	72	65	28-0	13	3	171	17.1
91-92	Bos.	4	107	21	42	.500	3	4	.750	2	16	18	21	7-0	1	2	45	11.3
TOTALS:		164	6886	1458	3090	.472	901	1012	.890	360	1323	1683	1062	466-1	296	145	3897	23.8

Three-Point Field Goals: 1979-80, 4-for-15 (.267); 1980-81, 3-for-8 (.375); 1981-82, 1-for-6 (.167); 1982-83, 1-for-4 (.250); 1983-84, 7-for-17 (.412); 1984-85, 7-for-25 (.280); 1985-86, 23-for-56 (.411), 1986-87, 14-for-41 (.341);1987-88, 12-for-32 (.375); 1988-89, 0-for-0 (.000); 1989-90, 5-for-19 (.263); 1990-91, 3-for-21 (.143); 1991-92, 0-for-5 (.000).
Totals: 80-for-249 (.321).

ALL STAR GAME RECORD

Year	Team	Min	FGM	FGA	Pct	FTM	FTA	Pct	Off	Def	Tot	Ast	PF-Dq	St	Bl	Pts	Avg
1980	Bos.	23	3	6	.500	0	0	.000	3	3	6	7	1-0	1	0	7	7.0
1981	Bos.	18	1	5	.200	0	0	.000	1	3	4	10	1-0	1	0	2	2.0
1982	Bos.	28	7	12	.583	5	8	.625	0	12	12	5	3-0	1	1	19	19.0
1983	Bos.	29	7	14	.500	0	0	.000	3	10	13	7	4-0	2	0	14	14.0
1984	Bos.	33	6	18	.333	4	4	1.000	1	6	7	3	1-0	2	0	16	16.0
1985	Bos.	31	8	16	.500	5	6	.833	5	3	8	2	3-0	0	1	21	21.0
1986	Bos.	35	8	18	.444	5	6	.833	2	6	8	5	5-0	7	0	23	23.0
1987	Bos.	35	7	18	.389	4	4	1.000	2	4	6	5	5-0	2	0	18	18.0
1988	Bos.	32	2	8	.250	2	2	1.000	0	7	7	1	4-0	4	1	6	6.0
1990	Bos.	23	3	8	.375	2	2	1.000	2	6	8	3	1-0	3	0	8	8.0
1991	Bos.	—selected, did not play due to back injury —															
1992	Bos.	—selected, did not play due to back injury —															
TOTALS:		287	52	123	.423	27	32	.844	19	60	79	41	28-0	23	3	134	13.4

Three-Point Field Goals: 1980, 1-for-2 (.500); 1983, 0-for-1 (.000); 1985, 0-for-1 (.000); 1986, 2-for-4 (.500); 1987, 0-for-3 (.000); 1988, 0-for-1 (.000); 1990, 0-for-1 (.000).
Totals: 3-for-13 (.231).

SEASON/CAREER HIGHS

	FGM	FGA	FTM	FTA	REB	AST	ST	BL	PTS
1991-92/Regular Season	19/22	35/36	14/16	14/17	19/21	12/17	4/9	2/5	49/60
1992/Playoffs	8/17	18/33	2/14	2/15	6/21	14/16	1/6	2/4	16/43

DEE BROWN   7

Position: Guard
Birthdate: November 29, 1968
Birthplace: Jacksonville, FL
High School: Bolles High (FL)
College: Jacksonville '90
Height: 6-1
Weight: 161
NBA Experience: 2 Years

HOW ACQUIRED: Celtics first-round draft choice in 1990... 19th pick overall.

1991-92 SEASON: Suffered a torn lateral meniscus of the left knee during practice on 10/29; had arthroscopic surgery the next day which revealed peripheral detachment of the lateral meniscus; placed on the IL on 10/31... practiced for the first time on 1/14... activated on 2/5 and played in his first game that night... recorded career highs of 23 points (10-16, 3-5) and 10 rebounds in just 29 minutes at Houston on 2/14; also had arguably his most spectacular dunk ever, and a splendid rebound over Hakeem Olajuwon... came off the bench in his first 11 appearances, before taking over a starter's role on 2/28 in Atlanta... dished out a career-high 14 assists that night, including an Omni record 10 in the first quarter... served out 35 assists in 3 games from 2/28-3/4... did not play at Milwaukee on 3/17 due to a left thigh bruise suffered on 3/15 vs. Portland... missed 5 games from 4/10-4/19 due to the flu... in 13 starts, he totalled 138 points (59-143, 1-9, 19-24) and 105 assists... 10+ minutes 31 times... 20+ minutes 29 times... 30+ minutes 11 times... 40+ minutes 4 times... 10+ points 21 times... 20+ points 2 times... 10+ rebounds once... 10+ assists 6 times... 5 double-doubles... **1992 Playoffs:** Missed the entire Indiana series as he was hampered by acute virus syndrome... played in all but Game 2 in the Cavaliers series... had 9 assists and 8 rebounds in Game 6 vs. Cleveland... made 7 of 11 field goals and scored 18 points in Game 7 at the Cavs... 10+ minutes 5 times... 20+ minutes 3 times... 10+ points 3 times.

PROFESSIONAL CAREER: Drafted by Boston on the first-round of the 1990 draft, the 19th pick overall... named to the 1991 NBA All-Rookie Team compiling the third highest point total behind Derrick Coleman and Lionel Simmons... gained instant notoriety by winning the Gatorade Slam Dunk Championship during the all-star weekend in Charlotte... was outstanding against Detroit in the 1991 playoff series; averaged 15.8 points and 5.3 assists in 31.5 minutes, and also made .534 (39-73) fgs... in Game Two vs. Detroit on 5/9/91, he tallied 15 fourth quarter points (22 overall) in a successful must-win situation.

COLLEGE CAREER: Named to the All-Sun Belt Conference Second Team as a junior; played predominantly at small forward... led the Dolphins in scoring (19.6 ppg), rebounding (7.6 rpg) and steals (56)... started 16 games at point guard and 13 at small forward as a senior; averaged 19.3 points, 5.0 assists, and 6.6 rebounds per game... finished as the ninth all-time scorer in Jax's history with 1,503 points, and finished second behind Ronnie Murphy with 201 steals... set team record for career three-pointers made with 87... field goal percentage and assists total increased each season... best season statistically was as a junior... set SBC Tournament record with 41

points vs. Old Dominion... named to the All-SBC First Team, and to the All-Tournament Team at the Orlando All-Star Classic in April, 1990.

PERSONAL: DeCovan Kadell Brown is single... a computer whiz, he has owned one since the age of eight... has designed his own computer programs... majored in math and computer science... has a younger sister and a younger brother... lists his dad as his most influential person... favorite basketball player was Julius Erving... favorite pregame meal is spaghetti, while his favorite meal is a cheeseburger... top musical performer is Janet Jackson... lists Orlando as his top NBA city (outside Boston)... lists "In Living Color" his top television show... works with the Easter Seals... lived in Jacksonville his entire life, before his move to Massachusetts where he lives year-round... shoe size is 14 and a half.

TOP REGULAR SEASON PERFORMANCES

Points
23 at Houston (2-14-92)
22 vs. Indiana at Htfd (3-4-91)
22 at Washington (3-15-91)
21 two times

Rebounds
10 at Houston (2-14-92)
6 vs. New Jersey (4-4-91)
6 vs. Dallas (3-1-92)
6 at Miami (3-28-91)
6 at Indiana (4-3-92)

Assists
14 at Atlanta (2-28-92)
11 vs. Orlando (3-4-92)
11 vs. Portland (3-15-92)
11 at Portland (3-10-91)

NBA RECORD

Year	Team	G	Min	FGM	FGA	Pct.	FTM	FTA	Pct.	Off	Def	Tot	Ast	PF-Dq	St	Bl	Pts	Avg
90-91	Bos.	82	1945	284	612	.464	137	157	.873	41	141	182	344	161-0	83	14	712	8.7
91-92	Bos.	31	883	149	350	.426	60	78	.769	15	64	79	164	74-0	33	7	363	11.7
TOTALS:		113	2828	433	962	.450	197	235	.838	56	205	261	508	235-0	116	21	1075	9.5

Three-Point Field Goals: 1990-91, 7-for-34 (.206); 1991-92, 5-for-22 (.227).Totals: 12-for-56 (.214).

PLAYOFF RECORD

90-91	Bos.	11	284	53	108	.491	28	34	.824	9	36	45	41	32-0	11	6	134	12.2
91-92	Bos.	6	120	22	44	.500	4	6	.667	3	9	12	31	16-2	1	4	48	8.0
TOTALS:		17	404	75	152	.493	32	40	.800	12	45	57	72	48-2	12	10	182	10.7

Three-Point Field Goals: 1990-91, 0-for-5 (.000); 1991-92, 0-for-3 (.000).Totals: 0-for-8 (.000).

SEASON/CAREER HIGHS

	FGM	FGA	FTM	FTA	REB	AST	ST	BL	PTS
1991-92/Regular Season	10/10	19/19	7/8	8/9	10/10	14/14	4/4	2/2	23/23
1992/Playoffs	6/9	13/14	4/8	6/10	8/9	9/10	1/2	1/1	18/22

SHERMAN DOUGLAS 20

Position: Guard
Birthdate: September 15, 1966
Birthplace: Washington, DC
High School: Spingarn High (DC)
College: Syracuse '89
Height: 6-0
Weight: 180
NBA Experience: 3 Years

HOW ACQUIRED: Traded by Miami to Boston for Brian Shaw on January 10, 1992.

1991-92 SEASON: Started the season as a restricted free agent with Miami; activated on 12/31 after signing an offer sheet with the Lakers on 12/13... appeared in 5 games with the Heat... acquired from Miami on 1/10 for Brian Shaw... in 3 games from 1/26-1/31, he totaled 78 minutes, 55 points (20-32, 15-20), 15 rebounds, and 16 assists... dished out a game-high 11 assists at Lakers on 2/14... recorded 4 straight games of 20+ minutes from 3/4-3/10... placed on the IL on 3/13 due to a sprained right ankle; activated on 3/22... returned to action on 3/29 after missing the previous 9 games... in 6 appearances from 4/7-4/19, he tallied 110 minutes, 50 points (22-44, 0-4, 6-13), 15 rebounds, and 35 assists... impressive in 27 minutes at Charlotte on 4/12, he recorded 12 points, 10 assists, 4 rebounds and 3 steals... 10+ minutes 32 times... 20+ minutes 15 times... 30+ minutes 2 times... 10+ points 10 times... 20+ points once... 10+ assists 2 times... one double-double... DNP-CD 5 times... wore number 20 in his first game as a Celtic, then switched to 4 until a shift back to 20 starting on 3/8... **1992 Playoffs:** Appeared in all 3 games against Indiana and in the first 3 games against Cleveland... 10+ minutes 5 times... DNP-CD 4 times.

PROFESSIONAL CAREER: Drafted by Miami on the second-round of the 1988 draft, the 28th pick overall... was named to the All-Rookie First Team... had the third highest scoring average (14.3) and was second in assists (7.6) among rookies in 1989-90... was the Heat's second highest scorer in 1989-90... started 65 times as a rookie after appearing as a reserve in the first 16... was selected Miami's MVP in 1990-91, a season in which he started every game and improved his numbers in scoring, assists, field goal and free throw percentages, rebounding and minutes.

COLLEGE CAREER: Left Syracuse as the NCAA's all-time leader in assists with 960... finished school as its all-time leader in scoring (2,060 points) and steals (235)... was the first player in Big East Conference history to lead the conference in assists three consecutive seasons... named First Team All-America by AP after senior season... scored 20 points (8-15, 2-2, 2-2) and added 7 assists in 1987 NCAA Finals loss to Indiana.

PERSONAL: Sherman Douglas (full name) is single... lists tennis and bowling as his hobbies... also enjoys playing baseball... close friends with former collegiate and professional teammate Rony Seikaly... lists Kevin Johnson as his toughest foe... favorite meal is steak and potatoes... shoe size is 11.

CAREER HIGHS: 42 points at Denver 12-27-90
7 rebounds vs. Atlanta 3-8-91
17 assists at Atlanta 2-26-90

TOP REGULAR SEASON PERFORMANCES (WITH CELTICS)

Points
20 at Milwaukee (1-31-92)
18 vs. Detroit (1-26-92)
17 at Washington (1-28-92)
16 vs. LA Clippers (3-6-92)

Rebounds
7 at Washington (1-28-92)
7 at Milwaukee (1-31-92)
4 at Charlotte (4-12-92)
4 at Philadelphia (4-14-92)

Assists
11 at LA Lakers (2-16-92)
10 at Charlotte (4-12-92)
8 vs. Milwaukee (4-10-92)
7 vs. New Jersey (1-15-92)

NBA RECORD

Year	Team	G	Min	FGM	FGA	Pct	FTM	FTA	Pct	Off	Def	Tot	Ast	PF-Dq	St	Bl	Pts	Avg
89-90	Miami	81	2470	463	938	.494	224	326	.687	70	136	206	619	187-0	145	10	1155	14.3
90-91	Miami	73	2562	532	1055	.504	284	414	.686	78	131	209	624	178-2	121	5	1352	18.5
91-92	Bos.	42	752	117	253	.462	73	107	.682	13	50	63	172	78-0	25	9	308	7.3
Totals:		196	5784	1112	2246	.495	581	847	.686	161	317	478	1415	443-2	291	24	2815	14.4

Three-Point Field Goals: 1989-90, 5-for-31 (.161); 1990-91, 4-for-31 (.129); 1991-92, 1-for-10 (.100). Totals: 10-for-72 (.139).

PLAYOFF RECORD

Year	Team	G	Min	FGM	FGA	Pct	FTM	FTA	Pct	Off	Def	Tot	Ast	PF-Dq	St	Bl	Pts	Avg
91-92	Bos.	6	65	9	25	.360	1	2	.500	1	3	4	10	8-0	0	0	19	3.2

Three-Point Field Goals: 1991-92, 0-for-2 (.000).

SEASON/CAREER HIGHS

	FGM	FGA	FTM	FTA	REB	AST	ST	BL	PTS
1991-92/Regular Season	7/15	12/26	6/13	10/17	7/7	11/17	2/6	2/2	20/42
1992/Playoffs	2/2	6/6	1/1	2/2	2/2	6/6	0/0	0/0	5/5

RICK FOX   44

Position: Guard/Forward
Birthdate: July 24, 1969
Birthplace: Toronto, Ontario
High School: Warsaw High (Warsaw, IN)
College: North Carolina '91
Height: 6-1
Weight: 231
NBA Experience: 1 Year

HOW ACQUIRED: Celtics first-round draft choice in 1991... 24th pick overall.

1991-92 SEASON: Boston's 1991 number one draft pick was selected by the league's head coaches to the All-Rookie Second Team... became the team's first rookie to start on opening night since Larry Bird in 1979... started the first five games; averaged 26.8 minutes, 12.2 points, 4.6 rebounds, and 1.8 assists, shot .522 (24-46) from the field and .765 (13-17) from the charity stripe... at New Jersey on 11/23, he registered 33 minutes, 25 points (11-13, 1-1, 2-4) and 5 rebounds... in 30 minutes at Atlanta on 11/30, he poured home a career-high 31 points (13-23, 4-7, 1-2)... tallied 5 points in 8 fourth quarter minutes in great comeback win vs. New York on 1/8... although he missed all 8 field goal attempts vs. San Antonio on 1/19, he yanked a season high 9 rebounds... fouled out in just 10 minutes at Miami on 3/10... played in the first 67 games, before a logging DNP-CD at Detroit on 3/20, the only time he did not play in a game this season... 10+ minutes 74 times... 20+ minutes 39 times... 30+ minutes 4 times (all in the season's first 16 games)... 10+ points 30 times... 20+ points 3 times... 30+ points once... DNP-CD once... **1992 Playoffs:** Played in every game except Games 2 and 3 against Cleveland... in Game 7 at Cavs, he made all 3 field goals, including a pair from 3-point land... 10+ minutes 3 times... DNP-CD 2 times.

COLLEGE CAREER: Tied a school record by playing in 140 games during his career; never missed a contest in four seasons... 13th all-time scorer at UNC with 1,703 points... all-time leader in steals with 197...scored a career best 26 points twice... named the team's MVP in his junior season... won the Butch Bennett Award as the team's most inspirational freshman player in 1987-88... as a frosh, he won the Mary Frances Andrews Award as the club's best field goal shooter... became the eighth player under Dean Smith to start in his first game, as the undermanned Carolina squad faced off against #1 Syracuse.

PERSONAL: Ulrick Fox is single... majored in Radio, Television and Motion Pictures... lists his hobby as golfing... favorite book is *The World's Greatest Salesman...* left Canada (born in Toronto, mother is from Trail, British Columbia) at the age of two; moved to Nassau, Bahamas where he lived with his parents Dianne, a Canadian 1964 Olympic high jumper, and Ulrich; moved to Indiana, where he played high school basketball, as part of a church mission sponsored program... shoe size is 14.

TOP REGULAR SEASON PERFORMANCES

Points	Rebounds	Assists
31 at Atlanta (11-30-91)	9 vs. San Antonio (1-19-92)	6 vs. Indiana (2-26-92)
25 at New Jersey (11-23-91)	8 vs. Milwaukee (4-10-92)	5 vs. New York (4-8-92)
21 at Chicago (12-25-91)	7 at Washington (11-2-91)	5 vs. Atlanta (3-29-92)
	5 at Sacr'to (11-12-91))	

NBA RECORD

Year	Team	G	Min	FGM	FGA	Pct	FTM	FTA	Pct	Off	Def	Tot	Ast	PF-Dq	St	Bl	Pts	Avg
91-92	Bos.	81	1535	241	525	.459	139	184	.755	73	147	220	126	230-3	78	30	644	8.0

Three-Point Field Goals:1991-92, 23-for-70 (.329).

PLAYOFF RECORD

Year	Team	G	Min	FGM	FGA	Pct	FTM	FTA	Pct	Off	Def	Tot	Ast	PF-Dq	St	Bl	Pts	Avg
91-92	Bos.	8	67	11	23	.478	4	4	1.000	3	3	6	4	11-0	2	2	29	3.6

Three-Point Field Goals:1991-92, 3-for-6 (.500).

SEASON/CAREER HIGHS

	FGM	FGA	FTM	FTA	REB	AST	ST	BL	PTS
1991-92/Regular Season	13/13	23/23	6/6	10/10	9/9	6/6	4/4	2/2	31/31
1992/Playoffs	3/3	9/9	2/2	2/2	2/2	2/2	1/1	2/2	8/8

KEVIN GAMBLE   34

Position: Guard/Forward
Birthdate: November 13, 1965
Birthplace: Springfield, IL
High School: Lanphier High (IL)
College: Iowa '87
Height: 6-5
Weight: 210
NBA Experience: 5 Years

HOW ACQUIRED: Signed as a free agent on December 15, 1988.

1991-92 SEASON: After sitting out the entire 1991 preseason, he came back into the fold before the regular season dawned... one of two (also Reggie Lewis) Celtics to play in every game... established career highs in rebounds and blocks... as a reserve, he chalked up 5 games, 18.4 minutes, 4.2 points, 2.0 rebounds, and 1.6 assists; he shot .346 (9-26) field goals, and .600 (3-5) free throws... regained his role as a starter on 11/10 and started every game since... tallied 21 points, 8 rebounds, and 6 assists in 34 minutes at Phoenix on 11/13... tabulated a career high 34 points (13-21, 8-8) vs. Sacramento on 1/6... since January, his numbers increased dramatically; thru December: 29 games, 727 (25.1) minutes, 279 points (9.6), and .502 (120-239) from the field; in the 28-game stretch of Larry Bird's absence: 988 (35.3) minutes, and 480 (17.1) points (204-398, 6-19, 66-71)... was a key on 3/15 vs. Portland as he hit 2 big free throws with 14.9 seconds left in the second overtime to give Boston a 4 point lead; also netted the game-tying basket at the buzzer of the first overtime... against Atlanta on 3/29, he tallied 22 points (11-14 field goals) and a season high tying 6 assists... at Charlotte on 4/12, he totalled 26 points (11-18, 4-6) and a career high 12 assists... in the last 7 games of the season, he logged 263 minutes, 121 points (54-92, 3-7, 10-12), 33 rebounds, and 22 assists... 10+ minutes 82 times... 20+ minutes 75 times... 30+ minutes 49 times... 40+ minutes 12 times... 10+ points 61 times... 20+ points 18 times... 30+ points 2 times... 10 rebounds once... 1 double-double... finished 8th in the NBA in free throw percentage and ranked 16th in field goal percentage; he was the only NBA player in the league to rank among the top 20 in both categories... **1992 Playoffs:** Started all 10 games... averaged 13.6 points, third highest on the squad... had 56 points and 18 rebounds in 3 games against Indiana... in Game 1 at Cleveland, he had 22 points and 6 rebounds... 10+ minutes 10 times... 20+ minutes 9 times... 30+ minutes 8 times... 40+ minutes 3 times... 10+ points 7 times... 20+ points 2 times.

PROFESSIONAL CAREER: Drafted by Portland on the third-round of the 1987 draft, the 63rd choice overall... began the 1987-88 season with the Blazers, playing nine games before being waived on December 9, 1987... joined the Quad City Thunder, and played in 40 games; he averaged 21.0 points, 5.9 rebounds, and 3.7 assists per game... finished third in the CBA Rookie of the Year voting... also played in the Phillines with Anejo Rum... during the summer of 1988, he played for the Chicago Express of the World Basketball League; he averaged 17.9 ppg and 5.9 rpg in 12 games (10 starts)... scored 33 points against Calgary in the 1988 WBL semifinals; he tallied 19 points and 9 boards in the final game loss to Las Vegas... in that WBL season, he shot 55.3% (84-152) from the floor, 38.9% (7-18) from 3-point range, and 80% (40-50) from the free throw line... in 1988-89, he continued his play with Quad City and was the CBA's leading scorer (27.8 ppg in 12 contests) before his promotion to the Celtics... had a great stretch in the last six games of 1988-89 in which he averaged 22.8 ppg; in 6 starts, he had 137 points (57-87, 0-4, 23-30) in 235 minutes while adding 29 assists and 28 rebounds... started Game One of the 1989 Celtics-Pistons opening round playoff series, but suffered a strained right groin which caused him to miss the remainder of the series... had 10 starts in 1989-90... improved most of his stats after his first four years... won the 1991 SportsChannel/Texaco Celtics Sixth Star Award given to the player who best represents Celtics pride... led the fg% category from 3/14/90-3/20/90 and finished 3rd in the NBA behind Portland's Buck Williams and teammate Robert Parish... fg% was as high as .625, at the all-star break... in the last 29 games before the 1991 all-star break, he made 223 of 337 fgs (.662).

COLLEGE CAREER: Played two years at Lincoln College in Lincoln, Illinois, and averaged 20.9 ppg... transferred to the University of Iowa, averaged 11.9 points and shot 54.4 percent from the field as a senior... played at Iowa under George Raveling and Tom Davis.

PERSONAL: Kevin Douglas Gamble is single... nicknamed "Oscar"... received an Associate's Degree in Law Enforcement... names Kareem Abdul-Jabbar as the greatest player he has ever seen... lists shopping, playing video games, golfing and fishing as his interests... likes rap music... returns to Illinois in the summer... fan of the St. Louis Cardinals... childhood hero was Julius Erving... shoe size is 14.

TOP REGULAR SEASON PERFORMANCES (WITH CELTICS)

Points
34 vs. Sacramento (1-6-92)
Philadelphia (4-18-91)
32 at New York (2-7-91)
31 vs. Charlotte (4-23-89)

Rebounds
12 at Charlotte (4-14-92)
10 at Charlotte (2-1-91)
9 vs. San Antonio (1-19-92)
9 at Orlando (4-6-91)

Assists
10 vs. Cleveland (4-14-89) 33 at
9 vs. Charlotte (11-14-90)
7 at Charlotte (4-17-89)
7 at Charlotte (12-20-90)

NBA RECORD

Year	Team	G	Min	FGM	FGA	Pct	FTM	FTA	Pct	Off	Def	Tot	Ast	PF-Dq	St	Bl	Pts	Avg
87-88	Por.	9	19	0	3	.000	0	0	.000	2	1	3	1	2-0	2	0	0	0.0
88-89	Bos.	44	375	75	136	.551	35	55	.636	11	31	42	34	40-0	14	3	187	4.3
89-90	Bos.	71	990	137	301	.455	85	107	.704	42	70	112	119	77-1	28	8	362	5.1
90-91	Bos.	82	2706	548	933	.587	185	227	.815	85	182	267	256	237-6	100	34	1281	15.6
91-92	Bos.	82	2496	480	908	.529	139	157	.885	80	206	286	219	200-2	75	37	1108	13.5
TOTALS:		288	6586	1240	2281	.543	444	546	.813	220	490	710	629	556-9	219	82	2938	10.2

Three-Point Field Goals: 1987-88, 0-for-1 (.000); 1988-89, 2-for-11 (.182);1989-90, 3-for-18 (.167); 1990-91, 0-for-7 (.000); 1991-92, 9-for-31 (.290).Totals: 14-for-68 (.206).

PLAYOFF RECORD

Year	Team	G	Min	FGM	FGA	Pct	FTM	FTA	Pct	Off	Def	Tot	Ast	PF-Dq	St	Bl	Pts	Avg
88-89	Bos.	1	29	4	11	.364	0	2	.000	1	0	1	2	1-0	1	0	8	8.0
89-90	Bos.	3	8	3	5	.600	0	0	.000	1	0	1	2	1-0	0	0	6	2.0
90-91	Bos.	11	238	29	60	.483	8	12	.667	3	10	13	19	24-0	4	2	66	6.0
91-92	Bos.	10	335	62	131	.473	12	15	.800	13	29	42	23	26-0	12	6	136	13.6
TOTALS:		25	610	98	202	.485	20	29	.690	18	39	57	46	52-0	17	8	216	8.6

Three-Point Field Goals: 1988-89, 0-for-1 (.000); 1991-92, 0-for-2 (.000).Totals: 0-for-3 (.000).

SEASON/CAREER HIGHS

	FGM	FGA	FTM	FTA	REB	AST	ST	BL	PTS
1991-92/Regular Season	14/16	24/25	8/9	8/12	12/12	6/10	3/5	2/3	34/34
1992/Playoffs	10/10	21/21	4/4	4/4	8/8	6/6	3/3	2/2	22/22

JOE KLEINE   53

Position: Center
Birthdate: January 4, 1962
Birthplace: Colorado Springs, CO
High School: Slater High (Slater, MO)
College: Arkansas '85
Height: 7-0
Weight: 271
NBA Experience: 7 Years

HOW ACQUIRED: Traded by Sacramento with Ed Pinckney to Boston for Danny Ainge and Brad Lohaus on February 23, 1989.

1991-92 SEASON: Established a career high field goal percentage... DNP-CD in the first 3 games ... started games on 11/13, 1/11, and 1/15; tallied 101 minutes, 26 points (12-21, 2-2) and 25 rebounds... made 10 straight field goals from 11/20-11/25... poured in 12 points (6-7 fgs) at Chicago in 18 minutes on 12/25... registered 4 rebounds and 2 points in 6 fourth quarter minutes vs. New York on 1/8 in key comeback win... established his Celtics career high with 40 minutes played at New York on 1/11... made 7 of 8 field goals vs. New Jersey on 1/15... entered the all-star break by tallying 10 or more points in three of the final four games ... played 24 minutes vs. Orlando on 3/4, tallied 15 points (7-10, 1-1, 0-0) and a season high 10 rebounds... entered this season 0-9 from 3-point range; finished 4-8 from that distance this season... his three-point field goal with 8.2 remaining at Utah on 2/17 was Boston's only field goal in a fourth quarter which saw the team shoot 1-for-19... did not play at Indiana on 4/3 due to a bruised left knee suffered vs. Washington on 4/1... 10+ minutes 47 times... 20+ minutes 15 times... 30+ minutes 3 times... 40+ minutes once... 10+ points 9 times... 10+ rebounds 3 times... 1 double-double... DNP-CD 11 times. **1992 Playoffs:** Saw action in every game except Game 4 vs. Cleveland... sharp outing in 22 minutes at Cavs in Game 5; tallied 12 points (6-10 fgs) and 11 rebounds... 10+ minutes 3 times... 20+ minutes once... 10+ rebounds once... 10+ points once... one double-double... DNP-CD once.

PROFESSIONAL CAREER: Drafted by Sacramento on the first-round of the 1985 draft, the sixth player taken overall... started 18 times in his rookie season... played in all 82 games in 1987-88, including starts in 60... was the Kings' second best rebounder in 1987-88... his minutes, field goals made, attempted, and percentage, free throws made, attempted, and percentage, offensive, defensive, and total rebounds, assists, blocks, points, and scoring average all increased in his first three years... missed just nine games in three-plus seasons with the Kings... in 1988-89, he started 11 times in 47 appearances for Sacramento... was a 92% free throw shooter in 1988-89 with Sacramento... was chosen the SportsChannel/Texaco Sixth Man of the Year for 1989-90... hit the game-winning field goal with 8.2 seconds left vs. Philadelphia on 3/11/90... started Game Six at Detroit on 5/17/91 (Robert Parish, injured).

COLLEGE CAREER: Played his freshman season with Notre Dame and made 64% of his fgs (32-50)... transferred to Arkansas... sat out the entire 1981-82 season... chosen Southwest Conference Newcomer of the Year in his first season with the Razorbacks, averaging 13.3 ppg in 1982-83... Arkansas' top scorer in his junior and senior years... ppg increased all four years... member of the 1984 US Olympic Team... member of the 1982 World University Games Team... graduated as the fourth best scorer in Arkansas' history (1,753).

PERSONAL: Joseph William Kleine and his wife Dana have two children, Daniel Christopher (2/23/89), born the day of his father's trade to Boston, and Courtney Frances (8/30/91)... college teammate of Alvin Robertson, Darrell Walker, Scott Hastings, and Tony Brown... likes to fish, golf, read and listen to country music... childhood heroes were Bill Walton and Dave Cowens... admires golfer Greg Norman... lists Dallas (besides Boston) as his favorite NBA city... usually returns to Dallas and Arkansas in the summer... graduated with a degree in Business Administration... shoe size is 16.

CAREER HIGHS: 23 points at LA Clippers 3-20-88
23 points vs. LA Clippers 4-2-88
18 rebs vs. Chicago 12-3-85
8 assists vs. LA Clippers 4-2-87

TOP REGULAR SEASON PERFORMANCES (WITH CELTICS)

Points	Rebounds	Assists
18 at Atlanta (3-13-90)	3 vs. Washington (1-3-90)	4 vs. Houston (3-31-89)
18 at Detroit (1-21-91)	12 at Chicago (11-4-89)	4 vs. Portland (3-29-89)
16 vs. Charlotte (2-7-90)	11 vs. Orlando (4-18-90)	4 at Atlanta (11-30-91)
16 vs. Houston (3-31-89)	11 vs. Houston (3-31-89)	3 three times

NBA RECORD

Year	Team	G	Min	FGM	FGA	Pct	FTM	FTA	Pct	Off	Def	Tot	Ast	PF-Dq	St	Bl	Pts	Avg
85-86	Sac.	80	1180	160	344	.465	94	130	.723	113	260	373	46	224-1	24	34	414	5.2
86-87	Sac.	79	1658	256	543	.471	110	140	.786	173	310	483	71	213-2	35	30	622	7.9
87-88	Sac.	82	1999	324	686	.472	153	188	.814	179	400	579	93	228-1	28	59	801	9.8
88-89	Sac/Bos	75	1411	175	432	.405	134	152	.882	124	254	378	67	192-0	33	23	484	6.5
89-90	Bos.	81	1365	176	367	.480	83	100	.830	117	238	355	46	170-0	15	27	435	5.4
90-91	Bos.	72	850	102	218	.468	54	69	.783	71	173	244	21	108-0	15	14	258	3.6
91-92	Bos.	70	991	144	293	.491	34	48	.708	94	202	296	32	99-0	23	14	326	4.7
TOTALS:		539	9454	1337	2883	.464	662	827	.800	871	1837	2708	376	1234-6	173	201	3340	6.2

Three-Point Field Goals:1986-87, 0-for-1 (.000); 1988-89, 0-for-2 (.000);1989-90, 0-for-4 (.000); 1990-91, 0-for-2 (.000); 1991-92, 4-for-8 (.500).Totals: 4-for-17 (.235).

PLAYOFF RECORD

Year	Team	G	Min	FGM	FGA	Pct	FTM	FTA	Pct	Off	Def	Tot	Ast	PF-Dq	St	Bl	Pts	Avg
85-86	Sac.	3	45	5	13	.385	5	6	.833	8	6	14	1	8-0	1	1	15	5.0
88-89	Bos.	3	65	6	11	.545	7	9	.778	4	13	17	2	9-0	0	1	19	6.3
89-90	Bos.	5	79	13	17	.765	5	6	.833	3	11	14	2	12-0	2	3	31	6.2
90-91	Bos.	5	31	4	9	.444	0	0	.000	5	6	11	1	7-0	2	0	8	1.6
91-92	Bos.	9	82	9	22	.409	2	2	1.00	6	16	22	1	11-0	0	1	20	2.2
TOTALS:		25	302	37	72	.513	19	23	.826	26	52	78	7	47-0	3	6	93	3.7

Three-Point Field Goals:1988-89, 0-for-1 (.000); 1989-90, 0-for-1 (.000); 1991-92, 0-for-1 (.000).Totals: 0-for-3 (.000).

SEASON/CAREER HIGHS

	FGM	FGA	FTM	FTA	REB	AST	ST	BL	PTS
1991-92/Regular Season	7/10	13/17	5/8	5/10	10/18	4/8	2/3	1/3	15/23
1992/Playoffs	6/6	10/10	2/6	2/7	11/11	1/1	0/1	1/1	12/12

REGGIE LEWIS   35

Position: Guard/Forward
Birthdate: November 21, 1965
Birthplace: Baltimore, MD
High School: Dunbar High (MD)
College: Northeastern '87
Height: 6-7
Weight: 195
NBA Experience: 5 Years

HOW ACQUIRED: Celtics first-round draft choice in 1987... 22nd pick overall.

1991-92 SEASON: His resplendent season was highlighted by being the lone Celtic to play in the 1992 All-Star Game... named as a reserve for the 1992 Eastern Conference All-Stars, his first appearance in the All-Star Game, and he registered 15 minutes, 7 points (3-7, 1-2), 4 rebounds, and 2 assists... was the 15th highest scorer per game in the league... was the lone Celtic to start each contest... became the first Celtic to lead the team in steals, blocks and points in the same season since Dave Cowens in 1977-78; in fact, Cowens' achievement is the only time a Celtic player has accomplished the feat... recorded many season-ending career highs... logged a career high-tying 5 blocks at Sacramento on 11/12... connected on 33 straight free throws from opening night to 11/13... on 11/25 vs. Washington, he recorded his third highest career point total with 37 (17-24, 3-5); the fgm was a career high... made 15 of 19 shots and scored 31 points on 12/9 vs. Denver... totalled 10+ points in 40 straight games from 12/4-2/26; under 10 points 2 times this season, both games at Atlanta... tallied 20+ points in 10 straight games from 1/4-1/22... in 28 games from 1/3-2/28 in Bird's absence, he recorded 1073 (38.3) minutes, 621 points (255-524, 3-12, 108-125), 33 points (14-22, 5-5)... in 39 minutes vs. New York on 1/8, he propelled Boston's win with 8 points in 10 fourth quarter minutes... attempted 20 or more shots in 5 straight games from 1/8-1/17... had at least one block in 16 straight games from 2/19-3/18... scored 29 points in key win at Detroit on 3/20... tremendous at Cleveland on 4/7 as he registered a game high and personal season high 38 points (17-27, 4-6); hit the game-winner with 11.8 seconds left and made all 8 field goals in the decisive fourth quarter... extraordinary at Charlotte on 4/12 as he compiled 35 points, including 15-19 field goals, 9 rebounds, 6 assists, 4 steals, and 3 blocks... named the NBA's Player of the Week for the period ending 4/12 with 28.0 points, 6.8 rebounds and 4.0 assists... 10+ points in the season's final 26 games...20+ points in 8 of the last 10 games... in the final 12 games, he registered 280 points (118-209, 44-55), 65 rebounds, and 41 assists in 621 minutes... 10+ minutes 82 times... 20+ minutes 82 times... 30+ minutes 80 times (under 20 minutes on 2/26 and 3/17)... 40+ minutes 31 times... 10+ points 80 times... 20+ points 46 times... 30+ points 9 times... 10+ rebounds once... 1 double-double... **1992 Playoffs:** Led Boston with 28.0 points, including a team best 28.1 points in 7

games against the Cavs and 27.7 in 3 games against Indiana... scored between 22 and 42 points in the last 6 games against Cleveland... in 48 minutes vs. Cleveland in Game 4, he logged a career high 42 points (16-28, 1-1, 9-12)... in Game 3 vs. the Cavs: 36 points (17-32, 0-1, 2-3) and 7 assists; added 13 points and 4 assists in the 4th quarter, and 13 points in the third quarter as he converted 12 of 20 field goals in the second half alone... against Indiana, he tallied 32 points in Game 3... 10+ minutes 10 times... 20+ minutes 10 times... 30+ minutes 10 times... 40+ minutes 6 times... 10+ points 10 times... 20+ points 8 times... 30+ points 4 times... 40+ points once.

PROFESSIONAL CAREER: Drafted by Boston on the first-round of the 1987 draft, the 22nd pick overall... saw limited duty in his first NBA season... best stretch in 1987-88 was a five game span from 11/15-11/21 as he scored 49 total points... in 1988-89, he started 57 times in the small forward position, replacing the injured Larry Bird... chosen the SportsChannel Sixth Man of the Year in 1988-89... finished second to Phoenix' Kevin Johnson in the NBA's Most Improved Player voting (1988-89), as he improved his scoring average from 4.5 to 18.5 and his minute total from 405 to 2657... started 54 times in 1989-90, establishing many career highs after his third season... set career bests in many statistical categories in 1990-91... started all 11 playoff games in 1991, and was Boston's leading scorer in both series at 22.4 points per outing... team leader with 28 points in Game One vs. Indiana on 4/26/91; also led the club in four games against Detroit in the 1991 playoffs, including a 30-point outing in Game Five.

COLLEGE CAREER: Four year starter at Northeastern... all-time Huskies leading scorer with 2,708 points (22.2); graduated as the ninth all-time NCAA Division One scorer... all-time leading shot blocker in Huskie history with 155... led Northeastern to four consecutive ECAC North Atlantic Conference titles as well as four straight trips to the NCAA Tournament... earned ECAC North Atlantic Conference Rookie of the Year honors... first ever three-time ECAC NAC Player of the Year, '85, '86, '87... the Huskies went 102-26 in his four years on Huntington Avenue, with a 72-6 conference record during that span... tri-captain in junior and senior years... had his jersey (number 35) retired in ceremonies on 1/21/89.

PERSONAL: Reggie Lewis is married to his college sweetheart, Donna Harris... played high school ball with NBA players Reggie Williams, Tyrone Bogues, and David Wingate; that team once went 50-0 in a season... considers his mom as the most influential person in his life... maintains residence year-round in the Boston area... signed on as a spokesperson with the Boys and Girls Clubs of Boston in an effort to teach youths the road to success is not paved with guns and drugs... as a youngster, he admired George Gervin... lists football and tennis as his favorite sports outside of basketball... shoe size is 13.

TOP REGULAR SEASON PERFORMANCES

Points
42 vs. New York (4-14-91)
39 at Philadelphia (3-28-89)
38 at Cleveland (4-7-92)
37 vs. Wash at Htfd (11-25-91)
35 vs. Portland (3-29-89)
35 at Charlotte (4-12-92)

Rebounds
12 at New York (1-18-91)
12 at Washington (1-12-91)
12 vs. Cleveland (4-14-89)
12 at Utah (3-13-91)
11 three times

Assists
9 vs. Orlando (4-18-90)
9 at LA Lakers (2-18-90)
8 vs. LA Clippers (1-5-90)
7 at Detroit (1-23-91)
7 vs. Chicago (4-5-92)

NBA RECORD

Year	Team	G	Min	FGM	FGA	Pct.	FTM	FTA	Pct.	Off	Def	Tot	Ast	PF-Dq	St	Bl	Pts	Avg
87-88	Bos.	49	405	90	193	.466	40	57	.702	28	35	63	26	54-0	16	15	220	4.5
88-89	Bos.	81	2657	604	1242	.486	284	361	.787	116	261	377	218	258-5	124	72	1495	18.5
89-90	Bos.	79	2522	540	1089	.496	256	317	.808	109	238	347	225	216-2	88	63	1340	17.0
90-91	Bos.	79	2878	598	1219	.491	281	340	.826	119	291	410	201	234-1	98	85	1478	18.7
91-92	Bos.	82	3070	703	1397	.503	292	343	.851	117	277	394	185	258-4	125	105	1703	20.8
TOTALS:		370	11532	2535	5140	.493	1153	1418	.813	489	1102	1591	855	1020-12	451	340	6236	16.9

Three-Point Field Goals:1987-88, 0-for-4 (.000); 1988-89, 3-for-22 (.136);1989-90, 4-for-15 (.267); 1990-91, 1-for-13 (.077);1991-92, 5-for-21 (.238).
Totals: 13-for-75 (.173).

PLAYOFF RECORD

Year	Team	G	Min	FGM	FGA	Pct.	FTM	FTA	Pct.	Off	Def	Tot	Ast	PF-Dq	St	Bl	Pts	Avg
87-88	Bos.	12	70	13	34	.382	3	5	.600	9	7	16	4	13-0	3	2	29	2.4
88-89	Bos.	3	125	26	55	.473	9	13	.692	5	16	21	11	11-0	5	0	61	20.3
89-90	Bos.	5	200	37	62	.597	27	35	.771	9	16	25	22	14-0	7	2	101	20.2
90-91	Bos.	11	462	95	195	.487	56	68	.824	18	50	68	32	33-1	12	6	246	22.4
91-92	Bos.	10	408	115	218	.528	48	63	.762	11	32	43	39	38-2	24	8	280	28.0
TOTALS:		41	1265	286	564	.507	143	184	.777	52	121	173	108	109-3	51	18	717	17.5

Three-Point Field Goals: 1987-88, 0-for-1 (.000); 1988-89, 0-for-2 (.000); 1989-90, 0-for-1 (.000); 1990-91, 0-for-4 (.000); 1991-92, 2-for-6 (.333).
Totals: 2-for-14 (.143).

ALL-STAR GAME RECORD

Year	Team	Min	FGM	FGA	Pct.	FTM	FTA	Pct.	Off	Def	Tot	Ast	PF-Dq	St	Bl	Pts	Avg
1992	Bos.	15	3	7	429	1	2	.500	4	0	4	2	3-0	0	1	7	7.0

SEASON/CAREER HIGHS

	FGM	FGA	FTM	FTA	REB	AST	ST	BL	PTS
1991-92/Regular Season	17/17	27/30	12/12	13/15	11/12	7/9	5/5	5/5	38/42
1992/Playoffs	17/17	32/32	9/9	12/12	6/11	7/9	5/5	2/2	42/42

KEVIN McHALE   32

Position: Forward/Center
Birthdate: December 19, 1957
Birthplace: Hibbing, MN
High School: Hibbing High (MN)
College: Minnesota '80
Height: 6-10
Weight: 225
NBA Experience: 12 Years

HOW ACQUIRED: Celtics first-round draft choice in 1980... 3rd pick overall.

1991-92 SEASON: The future hall of famer did not play in the preseason after a surgical procedure on 7/17 removed a bone spur and cleaned up ligament damage to the left ankle joint... appeared in the first 10 games of the season before a left ankle injury sidelined him for the next 9 games... started for the injured Larry Bird at New York on 12/15... played in 12 straight games from 12/13-1/4... missed 15 straight games from 1/6-2/5... had a bruised right calf, then strained it at practice on 1/13... placed on the IL before Boston's 1/15 game vs. New Jersey; an MRI on 1/15 confirmed a tear in the right calf muscle... activated from IL on 2/11... struggled in his first 3 games after his return, as he made just 3 of 19 field goals and scored 8 points... after that tough stretch in Texas, where all three games were played, he rebounded with a sumptuous effort at the Lakers by tallying 19 points and 8 rebounds in 29 minutes... experienced tightness in his left ankle area during practice on 3/3; did not dress in games on 3/4 and 3/6... Boston went 19-7 in his 26 missed games... made 19 of 23 (.826) field goals in consecutive games on 3/22 (Golden State) and 3/25 (New Jersey)... recorded 78 points in 4 games from 3/18-3/25... ended the season by making 91-158 (.576) from the field over the last 14 games... after the 3-19 total from the field in Texas, he concluded the campaign's last 31 games with 829 minutes (26.7), 488 points (15.7) (194-352, 0-6, 100-118), and 199 rebounds (6.4)... 10+ minutes 56 times... 20+ minutes 44 times... 30+ minutes 19 times... 10+ points 46 times... 20+ points 12 times... 10+ rebounds 8 times... 8 double-doubles... was named to the All-NBA Interview First Team in a vote conducted by a media panel; he received the third highest vote total... **1992 Playoffs:** Had 20+ point efforts in 3 of the final 5 games against Cleveland and was Boston's second leading scorer against the Cavs with 16.3 points per game... against Indiana, he averaged 32.0 minutes, 17.0 points, and 9.0 rebounds... 10+ minutes 10 times... 20+ minutes 10 times... 30+ minutes 7 times... 10+ rebounds once... 10+ points 9 times... 20+ points 4 times... 1 double-double.

PROFESSIONAL CAREER: Drafted by Boston on the first-round of the 1980 draft after Golden State took Joe Barry Carroll and Utah chose Darrell Griffith... is the third highest draft choice by Boston, behind 1947 #1 pick Ed Ehlers and 1986 #2 pick Len Bias...named to the NBA All-Rookie Team in 1981... preserved Boston's win in Game Six of Celtics-Sixers 1981 playoff series by blocking Andrew Toney's shot and then grabbing the rebound in the final seconds... started 32 times in the 1981-82 season... named to the All-Defensive Second Team in 1983, 1989, and 1990...

named to the All-Defensive First Team in 1986, 1987, and 1988... recipient of NBA's Sixth Man Award in 1984 and 1985... started 31 times in 1984-85, including 26 consecutive starts from 2/18-4/11... scored 56 points vs. Detroit on March 3, 1985 for what was then a team record... shares team record for field goals made in a game with 22... scored 42 points in New York in game following 56 point effort; 98 points in consecutive games is a team record... played in 413 consecutive games before missing on 12/21/84... in Game Four of the 1984 NBA Finals, his famous takedown of Kurt Rambis helped propel Boston to a win... became a starter in frontcourt when Celtics dealt Cedric Maxwell to the LA Clippers on 9/6/85... suffered a sore left Achilles in the 1985-86 season, causing him to miss 14 games... Boston's leading scorer in the 1985 and 1986 NBA Finals... 30+ points in 61 regular season games... became the first player in NBA history to shoot 60% from the floor and 80% from the free throw line in one season in 1986-87... became the fourth Celtic to register 2,000 points in a season when he accomplished that in 1986-87... finished among the NBA's top ten field goal shooters in each of the last six years, including first place finishes in 1986-87 and 1987-88... began the 1987-88 season on the injured list due to right foot surgery... scored the 10,000th point of his career on 1/12/88... hit a game-tying three-point goal with 5 seconds left in the first overtime of Game Two of the Celtics-Pistons Eastern Conference Finals (5/26/88)... became the eighth Celtic to grab 5,000 rebounds, on 2/1/89... was the only Celtic to play in all 82 games in 1989-90... scored 10+ points in 247 straight games; snapped on 11/18/89 at Detroit... had a career best free throw streak snapped at 44 on 12/13/89... in 1989-90, became the first player to finish in the top ten in fg% and ft% in the same season since Atlanta's Lou Hudson in 1969-70... starts by season: 1980-81 (1), 1981-82 (32), 1982-83 (13), 1983-84 (10), 1984-85 (31), 1985-86 (62), 1986-87 (77), 1987-88 (63), 1988-89 (74), 1989-90 (25), 1990-91 (10)... received the third highest vote total in the Miller Genuine Draft NBA Sixth Man Award balloting in 1990-91... missed 14 games due to a sprained left ankle in 1990-91... became the 54th NBA player to score 15,000 pts, accomplished on 12/19/90... was scintillating in Game Six at Detroit on 5/17/91 with a career playoff high-tying 34 points.

COLLEGE CAREER: First Team All-Big Ten selection by AP and UPI in 1979-80... graduated as Minnesota's second leading scorer (1,704 points) and rebounder (950)... team MVP in 1980... MVP of the Pillsbury Classic three times... MVP of the Aloha Classic in 1980... starter on the Gold Medal-winning Pan American Team in the summer of 1979... started on the Gold Medal-winning World University Games Team in 1979... named to the All-Big Ten Team for the 1970's.

PERSONAL: Kevin Edward McHale and his wife Lynn have four children, Kristyn (5/9/83), Michael (2/23/85), Joseph (12/10/86), and Alexandra (10/27/89)... favorite recreational sports are golfing and fishing; likes to play backgammon and read... is an ardent supporter of the Boston Bruins... returns to Minnesota in the summer... enjoys the music of Tom Petty, Bruce Springsteen and Hibbing, MN native Bob Dylan... was elected to the Minnesota State High School League Hall of Fame in April, 1992... appeared as himself twice on the television show "Cheers", the second time with his wife Lynn... shoe size is 15 and a half.

TOP REGULAR SEASON PERFORMANCES

Points
56 vs. Detroit (3-3-85)
42 at New York (3-5-85)
38 vs. Detroit (3-1-87)
38 vs. Cleveland (1-16-87)
37 two times

Rebounds
18 at LA Clippers (12-30-85)
18 at Detroit (1-16-89)
17 at Cleveland (1-23-88)
17 vs. Indiana (3-11-88)
17 vs. Golden State (11-21-86)

Assists
10 vs. Dallas (4-3-88)
9 vs. Philadelphia (3-25-88)
8 at New Jersey (4-9-86)
7 seven times

NBA RECORD

Year	Team	G	Min	FGM	FGA	Pct	FTM	FTA	Pct	Off	Def	Tot	Ast	PF-Dq	St	Bl	Pts	Avg
80-81	Bos.	82	1645	355	666	.533	108	159	.679	155	204	359	55	260-3	27	151	818	10.0
81-82	Bos.	82	2332	465	875	.531	187	248	.754	191	365	556	91	264-1	30	185	1117	13.6
82-83	Bos.	82	2345	483	893	.541	193	269	.717	215	338	553	104	241-3	34	192	1159	14.1
83-84	Bos.	82	2577	587	1055	.556	336	439	.765	208	402	610	104	243-5	23	126	1511	18.4
84-85	Bos.	79	2653	605	1062	.570	355	467	.760	229	483	712	141	234-3	28	120	1565	19.8
85-86	Bos.	68	2397	561	978	.574	326	420	.776	171	380	551	181	192-2	29	134	1448	21.3
86-87	Bos.	77	3060	790	1307	.604	428	512	.836	247	516	763	198	240-1	38	172	2008	26.1
87-88	Bos.	64	2390	550	911	.604	346	434	.797	159	377	536	171	179-1	27	92	1446	22.6
88-89	Bos.	78	2876	661	1211	.546	436	533	.818	223	414	637	172	223-2	26	97	1758	22.5
89-90	Bos.	82	2722	648	1181	.549	393	440	.893	201	476	677	172	250-3	30	157	1712	20.9
90-91	Bos.	68	2067	504	912	.553	228	275	.829	145	335	480	126	194-2	25	146	1251	18.4
91-92	Bos.	56	1398	323	634	.509	134	163	.822	119	211	330	82	112-1	11	59	780	13.9
TOTALS:		900	28444	6532	11685	.559	3470	4359	.796	2263	4501	6764	1597	2632-27	328	1631	16573	18.4

Three-Point Field Goals: 1980-81, 0-for-2 (.000); 1982-83, 0-for-1 (.000); 1983-84, 1-for-3 (.333); 1984-85, 0-for-6 (.000); 1986-87, 0-for-4 (.000); 1988-89, 0-for-4 (.000); 1989-90, 23-for-69 (.333); 1990-91, 15-for-37 (.405); 1991-92, 0-for-13 (.000).
Totals: 39-for-139 (.281).

PLAYOFF RECORD

Year	Team	G	Min	FGM	FGA	Pct	FTM	FTA	Pct	Off	Def	Tot	Ast	PF-Dq	St	Bl	Pts	Avg
80-81	Bos.	17	296	61	113	.540	23	36	.639	29	30	59	14	51-1	4	25	145	8.5
81-82	Bos.	12	344	77	134	.575	40	53	.755	41	44	85	11	44-0	5	27	194	16.2
82-83	Bos.	7	177	34	62	.548	10	18	.556	15	27	42	5	16-0	3	7	78	11.1
83-84	Bos.	23	702	123	244	.504	94	121	.777	62	81	143	27	75-1	3	35	340	14.8
84-85	Bos.	21	837	172	303	.568	121	150	.807	74	134	208	32	73-3	13	46	465	22.1
85-86	Bos.	18	715	168	290	.579	112	141	.794	51	104	155	48	64-0	8	43	448	24.9
86-87	Bos.	21	827	174	298	.584	96	126	.762	66	128	194	39	71-2	7	30	444	21.1
87-88	Bos.	17	716	158	262	.603	115	137	.839	55	81	136	40	65-1	7	30	432	25.4
88-89	Bos.	3	115	20	41	.448	17	23	.739	7	17	24	9	13-0	1	2	57	19.0
89-90	Bos.	5	192	42	69	.609	25	29	.862	8	31	39	13	17-0	2	10	110	22.0
90-91	Bos.	11	376	78	148	.527	66	80	.825	18	54	72	20	42-0	5	14	228	20.7
91-92	Bos.	10	306	65	126	.516	35	44	.795	21	46	67	13	34-0	5	5	165	16.5
TOTALS:		165	5603	1172	2090	.561	754	958	.787	447	777	1224	271	565-8	63	274	3106	18.8

Three-Point Field Goals: 1982-83, 0-for-1 (.000); 1983-84, 0-for-3 (.000); 1985-86, 0-for-1 (.000); 1987-88, 1-for-1 (1.000); 1989-90, 1-for-3 (.333); 1990-91, 6-for-11 (.545); 1991-92, 0-for-1 (.000). Totals: 8-for-21 (.381).

ALL STAR RECORD

Year	Team	Min	FGM	FGA	Pct	FTM	FTA	Pct	Off	Def	Tot	Ast	PF-Dq	St	Bl	Pts	Avg
1984	Bos.	11	3	7	.429	4	6	.667	2	3	5	0	1-0	0	0	10	10.0
1986	Bos.	20	3	38	.375	2	2	1.000	3	7	10	2	4-0	0	4	8	8.0
1987	Bos.	30	7	11	.636	2	2	1.000	4	3	7	2	5-0	0	4	16	16.0
1988	Bos.	14	0	1	.000	2	2	1.000	0	1	1	1	2-0	0	2	2	2.0
1989	Bos.	16	5	7	.714	0	0	.000	`1	2	3	0	3-0	0	2	10	10.0
1990	Bos.	20	6	11	.545	0	0	.000	2	6	8	1	4-0	0	0	13	13.0
1991	Bos.	14	0	3	.000	2	2	1.000	1	2	3	2	2-0	1	0	2	2.0
TOTALS:		125	24	48	.500	12	14	.857	13	24	37	8	21-0	1	12	61	8.7

Three-Point Field Goals: 1990, 1-for-1 (1.000); 1991, 0-for-1 (.000). Totals: 1-for-2 (.500).

SEASON/CAREER HIGHS

	FGM	FGA	FTM	FTA	REB	AST	ST	BL	PTS
1991-92/Regular Season	10/22	21/30	10/15	10/19	12/18	5/10	1/3	4/9	26/56
1992/Playoffs	10/15	15/25	11/14	11/16	11/17	3/7	1/3	1/6	23/34

ROBERT PARISH   00

Position: Center
Birthdate: August 30, 1953
Birthplace: Shreveport, LA
High School: Woodlawn High (LA)
College: Centenary '76
Height: 7 feet, half inch
Weight: 230
NBA Experience: 16 Years

HOW ACQUIRED: Traded by Golden State with a 1980 first-round draft choice for two 1980 first-round draft choices on June 9, 1980.

1991-92 SEASON: 1991-92 was a season of milestones for the NBA's oldest active player as this colossal talent tallied his 20,000th point (16th in NBA history) on 1/17 vs. Philadelphia, 12,000th rebound (8th player in NBA history to total both 20,000 points and 10,000 rebounds) and 1,000th steal vs. Charlotte on 11/1, 1200 game played (5th player in NBA history) on 12/13 vs. Seattle, and 2,000th block (5th player in NBA history) on 1/4 at Minnesota; other than the steals figure, he is the 2nd player in NBA annals to reach the other four figures, joining Kareem Abdul-Jabbar... the Basketball Hall of Fame dedicated a display case for these milestones with an exhibit in early 1992... the exceptionally conditioned athlete missed just 3 games with injuries... in a 6-game span from 11/23-12/4, he connected on 41 of 56 field goals (.732)... on 12/4 vs. Miami, he recorded 31 points, made 13 of 16 field goals, and blocked 4 shots... was severely missed after suffering a sprained left ankle vs. Minnesota on 1/10, in which he had 22 points and 9 rebounds in just 23 minutes; with him out of the lineup, Boston blew a lead to the Timberwolves and lost the next two games, at New York (1/11) and home to New Jersey (1/15), in his absence... superb vs. San Antonio on 1/19, as he totalled game highs with 30 points (12-22, 6-7) and 14 rebounds... signed a contract extension on 2/11, through the 1992-93 season... like the previous season, he led the Celtics to a win at the Lakers; on 2/16, he made all 9 first half field goal attempts and ended the night with 21 points (10-12 fgs) and 11 rebounds... tallied five straight double-doubles from 2/16-2/21... made all 12 field goal attempts against Atlanta in the last two meetings with the Hawks, 3/29 (5-5) and 2/28 (7-7)... from 1/26 to the end of the season, he attempted 19 field goals 3 times, all were against Detroit... for the second straight season, he played an instrumental role in the Celtics division title clincher, as he grabbed a season high 19 rebounds and tallied 22 points vs. Miami on 4/19... 10+ minutes 79 times... 20+ minutes 76 times... 30+ minutes 38 times... 40+ minutes 5 times... 10+ points 61 times... 20+ points 15 times... 30+ points 2 times... 10+ rebounds 32 times... 28 double-doubles... finished 14th in the league among field goal percentage and ranked 20th in rebounds per game... **1992 Playoffs:** Averaged 12.0 points in 10 games, fourth highest on the team... in 47 minutes in Game 4 vs. Cleveland, he totalled game highs with 18 rebounds and 3 blocks and scored 16 points... led all players with 17 rebounds in Game 3 vs. Cleveland... scored a game high 27 points in 42 minutes at Cavs in Game 2 after totalling 6 points in the previous 2 games... in 3 games against Indiana, he averaged 38.3 minutes, 14.7 points, and 11.7 rebounds... 10+ minutes 10 times... 20+ minutes 10 times... 30+ minutes 6 times... 40+ minutes 3 times... 10+ rebounds 4 times... 10+ points 6 times... 20+ points 2 times... 4 double-doubles.

PROFESSIONAL CAREER: Drafted by Golden State on the first-round of the 1976 draft, the 8th pick overall... had an incredible game on 3/30/79 vs. New York when he scored 30 points and grabbed 32 rebounds... played his first four professional seasons in Oakland, then was involved in a blockbuster trade to Boston along with a first-round pick used to select Kevin McHale; in return, Boston traded two number one picks (Detroit's at #1, and Washington's at #13) to Golden State, which selected Joe Barry Carroll and Rickey Brown... became Boston's starting center when Dave Cowens suddenly retired... runner-up to Larry Bird in the 1982 all-star MVP balloting... shares the team record with 9 blocks on 3/17/82... holds the team playoff record with 7 blocks on 5/9/82... named to the All-NBA Second Team in 1982... scored the 10,000th point of his career on 2/26/84 in Phoenix... had two key steals in the waning moments of overtime in Game Two of the 1984 Finals... played in 99 of 100 games in the 1985-86 season... is the only Celtic to grab 25+ rebounds in a game (accomplished twice) since the 1977-78 season... registered his lone triple-double on 3/29/87 vs. the Sixers... missed Game Six of the 1987 series at Milwaukee due to an injured left ankle, snapping a streak of 116 straight playoff appearances... did not play on 5/28/87, serving a one game suspension for punching Bill Laimbeer in the previous game... finished second to teammate Kevin McHale in field goal accuracy during the 1987-88 season; in fact, he has been in the NBA's top ten in each of the past seven years... grabbed his 10,000th rebound on 2/22/89... named to the All-NBA Third Team in 1989... scored his 18,000th point on 3/7/90... established career highs in field goal percentage and free throw percentage in 1990-91 and finished second to Portland's Buck Williams in field goal percentage... his buzzer-beating game-winning jumpshot on 3/29/91 vs. Cleveland enabled Boston to declare the division title... tallied 21 first quarter points at LAL on 2/15/91, including his 19,000th career point... led the Celtics in field goal shooting (.598) and rebounding per game (9.2) during his ten 1991 playoff appearances; missed Game Six at Detroit due to a sprained left ankle.

COLLEGE CAREER: Named to The Sporting News All-America First Team in 1976... a Gold Medalist in the 1975 World University Games, a team coached by Dave Gavitt... played four years at Centenary... once had 50 points in a game against Southern Miss... grabbed 33 rebounds in a game... averaged 21.6 points in 108 career games... averaged 23.0 points as a freshman, and 24.8 as a senior... made 56.4% of his fgs.

PERSONAL: Robert Lee Parish is single... enjoyments include judo, racquetball, backgammon, jazz music, viewing boxing, the works of Stephen King and horror films... nicknamed "Chief" by Cedric Maxwell, after Chief Bromden in "One Flew Over the Cuckoo's Nest"... resides in the Boston area year-round... went to the same high school as former Pittsburgh Steelers' star Terry Bradshaw... lists the 1981 championship as his most memorable moment in basketball... names Bill Russell, Wilt Chamberlain, and Clifford Ray as his favorite athletes... participated in the Robert Parish/Dee Brown All-Star Basketball Camp in the summer of 1992... shoe size is 16.

CAREER HIGHS: 32 rebounds vs. New York 3-30-79

TOP REGULAR SEASON PERFORMANCES (WITH CELTICS)

PPoints
40 at San Antonio (2-17-81)
38 vs. Houston (3-17-85)
38 vs. Denver (12-8-89)
37 at Philadelphia (3-21-82)

Rebounds
25 vs. Sacramento (1-9-87)
25 at Washington (3-8-86)
24 at Charlotte (2-1-89)
23 two times

Assists
10 vs. Philadelphia (3-29-87)
9 at Detroit (11-15-86)
7 at Chicago (1-21-83)
7 vs. Seattle (2-5-89)

NBA RECORD

Year	Team	G	Min	FGM	FGA	Pct	FTM	FTA	Pct	Off	Def	Tot	Ast	PF-Dq	St	Bl	Pts	Avg
76-77	G.S.	77	1384	288	573	.503	121	171	.708	201	342	543	74	224-7	55	94	697	9.1
77-78	G.S.	82	1969	430	911	.472	165	264	.625	211	469	680	95	291-10	79	123	1025	12.5
78-79	G.S.	76	2411	554	1110	.499	196	281	.698	265	651	916	115	303-10	100	217	1304	17.2
79-80	G.S.	72	2119	510	1006	.507	203	284	.715	247	536	783	122	248-6	58	115	1223	17.0
80-81	Bos.	82	2298	635	1166	.545	282	397	.710	245	532	777	144	310-9	81	214	1552	19.9
81-82	Bos.	80	2534	669	1235	.542	252	355	.710	288-	578	866	140	267-5	68	192	1590	19.9
82-83	Bos.	78	2459	619	1125	.550	271	388	.698	260	567	827	141	222-4	79	148	1509	19.3
83-84	Bos.	80	2867	623	1140	.546	274	368	.745	243	614	857	139	266-7	55	116	1520	19.0
84-85	Bos.	79	2850	551	1016	.542	292	393	.743	263	577	840	125	223-2	56	101	1394	17.6
85-86	Bos.	81	2567	530	966	.549	245	335	.731	246	524	770	145	215-3	65	116	1305	16.1
86-87	Bos.	80	2995	588	1057	.556	227	309	.735	254	597	851	173	266-5	64	144	1403	17.5
87-88	Bos.	74	2312	442	750	.589	177	241	.734	173	455	628	115	198-5	55	84	1061	14.3
88-89	Bos.	80	2840	596	1045	.570	294	409	.719	342	654	996	175	209-2	79	116	1486	18.6
89-90	Bos.	79	2396	505	871	.580	233	312	.747	259	537	796	103	189-2	38	69	1243	15.7
90-91	Bos.	81	2441	485	811	.598	237	309	.767	271	585	856	66	197-1	66	103	1207	14.9
91-92	Bos.	79	2285	468	874	.535	179	232	.772	219	486	705	70	172-2	68	97	1115	14.1
TOTALS:		1260	38727	8493	15656	.542	3648	5043	.723	3987	8704	12691	1942	3800-80	1066	2049	20634	16.4

Three-Point Field Goals: 1979-80, 0-for-1 (.000); 1980-81, 0-for-1 (.000); 1982-83, 0-for-1 (.000); 1986-87, 0-for-1 (.000); 1987-88 0-for-1 (.000); 1990-91, 0-for-1 (.000). Totals: 0-for-6 (.000).

PLAYOFF RECORD

Year	Team	G	Min	FGM	FGA	Pct	FTM	FTA	Pct	Off	Def	Tot	Ast	PF-Dq	St	Bl	Pts	Avg
76-77	G.S.	10	239	52	108	.481	17	26	.654	43	60	103	11	42-1	7	11	121	12.1
80-81	Bos.	17	492	108	219	.493	39	58	.672	50	96	146	19	74-2	21	39	255	15.0
81-82	Bos.	12	426	102	209	.488	51	75	.680	43	92	135	18	47-1	5	48	255	21.3
82-83	Bos.	7	249	43	89	.483	17	20	.850	21	53	74	9	18-0	5	9	103	14.7
83-84	Bos.	23	869	139	291	.478	64	99	.646	76	172	248	27	100-6	23	41	342	14.9
84-85	Bos.	21	803	136	276	.493	87	111	.784	57	162	219	31	68-0	21	34	359	17.1
85-86	Bos.	18	591	106	225	.471	58	89	.652	52	106	158	25	47-1	9	30	270	15.0
86-87	Bos.	21	734	149	263	.567	79	103	.767	59	139	198	28	79-4	18	35	377	18.0
87-88	Bos.	17	626	100	188	.532	50	61	.820	51	117	168	21	42-0	11	19	250	14.7
88-89	Bos.	3	112	20	44	.455	7	9	.778	6	20	26	6	5-0	4	2	47	15.7
89-90	Bos.	5	170	31	54	.574	17	18	.944	23	27	50	13	21-0	5	7	79	15.8
90-91	Bos.	10	296	58	97	.598	42	61	.689	33	59	92	6	34-1	8	7	158	15.8
91-92	Bos.	10	335	50	101	.495	20	28	.714	38	59	97	14	22-0	7	15	120	12.0
TOTALS:		174	5942	1094	2164	.506	548	758	.723	552	1162	1714	228	599-16	144	297	2736	15.7

Three-Point Field Goals: 1986-87, 0-for-1 (.000).

ALL STAR GAME RECORD

Year	Team	Min	FGM	FGA	Pct	FTM	FTA	Pct	Off	Def	Tot	Ast	PF-Dq	St	Bl	Pts	Avg
1981	Bos.	25	5	18	.278	6	6	1.000	6	4	10	2	3-0	0	2	16	16.0
1982	Bos.	20	9	12	.750	3	4	.750	0	7	7	1	2-0	0	2	21	21.0
1983	Bos.	18	5	6	.833	3	4	.750	0	3	3	0	2-0	1	1	13	13.0
1984	Bos.	28	5	11	.455	2	4	.500	4	11	15	2	1-0	3	0	12	12.0
1985	Bos.	10	2	5	.400	0	0	.000	3	3	6	1	0-0	0	0	4	4.0
1986	Bos.	7	0	0	.000	0	2	.000	0	1	1	0	0-0	0	1	0	0.0
1987	Bos.	8	2	3	.667	0	0	.000	0	3	3	0	1-0	0	1	4	4.0
1990	Bos.	21	7	11	.636	0	1	.000	2	2	4	2	4-0	0	1	14	14.0
1991	Bos.	5	1	2	.500	0	0	.000	1	3	4	0	2-0	0	0	2	2.0
TOTALS:		142	36	68	.529	14	21	.667	16	37	53	8	15-0	4	8	86	9.6

Three-Point Field Goals: None attempted.

SEASON/CAREER HIGHS

	FGM	FGA	FTM	FTA	REB	AST	ST	BL	PTS
1991-92/Regular Season	13/16	26/31	10/13	10/18	19/32	4/10	3/6	5/9	31/40
1992/Playoffs	13/14	16/25	7/11	10/15	18/19	5/6	2/5	4/7	27/33

ED PINCKNEY   54

Position: Forward
Birthdate: March 27, 1963
Birthplace: Bronx, NY
High School: Adlai Stevenson High (NY)
College: Villanova '85
Height: 6-9
Weight: 215
NBA Experience: 7 Years

HOW ACQUIRED: Traded by Sacramento with Joe Kleine to Boston for Danny Ainge and Brad Lohaus on February 23, 1989.

1991-92 SEASON: The electrifying performer was hailed as the SportsChannel Sixth Man Award Winner as voted by fans to the player whose contributions to the team best represents Celtic Pride... came off the bench in every game in November and December before replacing the injured Larry Bird for all of January and February... got off to a blistering start as he connected .680 (17-25) of his field goals after the first 7 games... in 4 games from 11/30-12/9, he logged 90 minutes (22.5), 54 points (17-26, 20-20) and 35 rebounds (8.8)... in 10 games from 11/30-12/21, he recorded 81 rebounds (8.1) and 111 points (11.1); he entered the 11/30 game with 3.9 rpg and 5.6 ppg... played in every game but Christmas Day at Chicago, due to a sore right foot... vs. New York on 1/8, he grabbed 8 rebounds and scored 4 points in 12 fourth quarter minutes to aid Boston in their comeback win... as a starter in the place of Bird, he totalled 36 games, 1058 (29.4) minutes, 290 (8.1) points (100-185, 90-113) and 309 rebounds (8.6)... grabbed 48 rebounds in 3 games from 2/19-2/23... had a fine outing on 2/26 vs. Indiana as he recorded 37 minutes, 10 rebounds, 12 points, 2 blocks and a career high 7 steals... in a 3-game spread from 3/4-3/8, he blocked 9 shots... vs. Portland on 3/15, all 6 of his points came in the second overtime, including the go-ahead hoop with 3:03 left... grabbed 14 or more rebounds in 7 different games; had just 3 such efforts as a Celtic entering this season... 10+ minutes 75 times... 20+ minutes 50 times... 30+ minutes 25 times... 40+ minutes 2 times... 10+ points 28 times... 10+ rebounds 18 times... 9 double-doubles... **1992 Playoffs:** Was the team's second leading rebounder with 8.4 per game... started 8 of the 10 games, exceptions were the last 2 games against Cleveland... made 28 of 44 field goals (.636) in 7 games against

the Cavs... had perhaps the best playoff game of his career with a career high 17 points (5-7, 7-7) and 13 rebounds in 39 minutes against Cleveland in Game 3... against Indiana, he averaged in 31.3 minutes, 10.0 rebounds and 8.3 points... 10+ minutes 10 times... 20+ minutes 9 times... 30+ minutes 6 times... 40+ minutes 2 times... 10+ rebounds 4 times... 10+ points 6 times... 2 double-doubles.

PROFESSIONAL CAREER: Drafted by Phoenix on the first-round of the 1985 draft, the 10th pick overall... played his first two professional seasons with the Suns... traded to the Kings on June 21, 1987, along with a 1988 second-round draft choice in exchange for Eddie Johnson... had seven starts in the 1987-88 season... led the Kings in field goal percentage in 1987-88 (.522)... played 54 games with the Kings in 1988-89, including 24 starts... led Sacramento by shooting 50.2% in 1988-89 before the trade to Boston... started nine times in his initial season with Boston... started 50 times in 1989-90... had 16 points in 14 minutes in Game Two of the 1990 playoff opener against New York... made 14 straight field goals from 3/28-4/4, and 23 of 30 (.767) over 8 games from 3/22-4/11... posted a dazzling field goal percentage in the 1991 playoffs; shot .762 (16-21) from the floor in 11 outings... was a key figure in Boston's incredible comeback run in Game Six at Detroit on 5/17/91, as he was one of five players who fought back from an 80-65 deficit without substitution until the overtime's last 12 seconds.

COLLEGE CAREER: Member of the 1985 NCAA Champions... chosen MVP of the NCAA Division One Tournament in 1985... honorable mention All-America as a sophomore, junior, and senior... led the Wildcats in blocks, rebounds, and fg% all four years... 1983 Gold Medal-winner in the Pan American Games... graduated as Villanova's fifth best scorer (1,865), fourth best rebounder (1,107), and top field goal shooter (.604)... remarkably, his lowest fg% was .568 as a sophomore.

PERSONAL: Edward Lewis Pinckney and his wife Rose have two children, Shea (11/5/84) and Spence (8/22/88)... has seven sisters... involved in many charitable causes... favorite NBA city (outside Boston) is New York... likes former NBA great Julius Erving... graduated with a degree in Communications... likes playing softball and handball... lives in New Jersey during the summer... shoe size is 13.

CAREER HIGHS: 27 points vs. Seattle 3-26-86
6 assists vs. Houston 4-1-87

TOP REGULAR SEASON PERFORMANCES (WITH CELTICS)

Points	Rebounds	Assists
22 vs. San Antonio (3-20-89)	18 vs Char at Htfd (2-21-92)	6 at Indiana (3-16-89)
22 vs. Portland (3-29-89)	7 at Orlando (4-6-91)	5 at Detroit (3-17-89)
19 vs. New York (3-24-89)	16 vs. Houston (2-5-92)	5 at Orlando (1-17-90)
19 vs. Chicago (4-20-89)	16 at Indiana (2-23-92)	5 vs. Chicago (11-9-90)
19 vs. Orlando (1-30-91)	15 at Minnesota (1-28-91)	
19 vs. Cleveland (3-29-91)		

NBA RECORD

Year	Team	G	Min	FGM	FGA	Pct	FTM	FTA	Pct	Off	Def	Tot	Ast	PF-Dq	St	Bl	Pts	Avg
85-86	Pho.	80	1602	255	457	.558	171	254	.673	95	213	308	90	190-3	71	37	681	8.5
86-87	Pho.	80	2250	290	497	.584	257	348	.739	179	401	580	116	196-1	86	54	837	10.5
87-88	Sac.	79	1177	179	343	.522	133	178	.747	94	136	230	66	118-0	39	32	491	6.2
88-89	Sac/Bos	80	2012	319	622	.513	280	350	.800	166	283	449	118	202-2	83	66	918	11.5
89-90	Bos.	77	1082	135	249	.542	92	119	.773	93	132	225	68	126-1	34	42	362	4.7
90-91	Bos.	70	1165	131	243	.539	104	116	.897	155	186	341	45	147-0	61	43	366	5.2
91-92	Bos.	81	1917	203	378	.537	207	255	.812	252	312	564	62	158-1	70	56	613	7.6
TOTALS:		547	11205	1512	2789	.542	1244	1620	.768	1034	1663	2697	565	1137-8	444	330	4268	7.8

Three-Point Field Goals: 1985-86, 0-for-2 (.000); 1986-87, 0-for-2 (.000); 1987-88, 0-for-2 (.000); 1988-89, 0-for-6 (.000); 1989-90, 0-for-1 (.000); 1990-91, 0-for-1 (.000); 1991-92, 0-for-1 (.000).Totals: 0-for-15 (.000).

PLAYOFF RECORD

Year	Team	G	Min	FGM	FGA	Pct	FTM	FTA	Pct	Off	Def	Tot	Ast	PF-Dq	St	Bl	Pts	Avg
88-89	Bos.	3	112	20	44	.455	7	9	.778	6	20	26	6	5-0	4	2	47	15.7
89-90	Bos.	4	25	6	7	.857	7	9	.778	2	4	6	0	3-0	0	0	19	4.8
90-91	Bos.	11	170	16	21	.762	17	21	.810	23	17	40	2	17-0	6	2	49	4.5
91-92	Bos.	10	314	35	58	.603	26	31	.839	36	48	84	7	30-0	12	9	96	9.6
TOTALS:		28	554	60	98	.612	52	63	.825	63	72	135	10	57-0	19	12	172	6.1

Three-Point Field Goals: 1991-92, 0-for-1 (.000).

SEASON/CAREER HIGHS

	FGM	FGA	FTM	FTA	REB	AST	ST	BL	PTS
1991-92/Regular Season	6/10	10/16	10/12	11/15	18/18	4/6	7/7	4/4	17/27
1992/Playoffs	5/6	9/9	7/8	8/8	14/14	2/2	4/4	2/2	17/17

RED AUERBACH

PRESIDENT

For the first four years of its existence, the Boston Celtics were a struggling operation at best, losing six times in every ten outings. Team Owner Walter Brown decided it would take a unique person, one of ingenuity and determination to steer the fortunes of his team. The search concluded with Red Auerbach, previously the Head Coach of the Washington Capitols and Tri-Cities Hawks. Although the Celtics were competitive for the first six years of his regime, the NBA championship still eluded the franchise.

On April 20, 1956, Auerbach engineered an historic transaction by trading Ed Macauley and Cliff Hagan to St. Louis for the Hawks first-round pick who would be Bill Russell. This blockbuster move would spur the Celtics into the most dominant franchise in pro basketball history. Auerbach, who is still the winningest coach in NBA annals, coached the Celtics to nine NBA championships, including eight in succession from 1959-1966. Upon retiring as the team's Head Coach, Auerbach concentrated singularly on his duties as General Manager.

With his guidance and knowledge, the Celtics continued to win. In 1968 and 1969, the Celtics added two more titles. But after a down period in the early 70s, Auerbach restructured the team adding key personnel through trades and the draft, and ultimately raised banners in 1974 and 1976. It was after these years that Auerbach would have his toughest test, as the late 1970s were a dismal period for the Celtics. Yet, Auerbach once again saved the franchise with the shrewd selection of Larry Bird in the 1978 draft. Although he would have to wait a year before Bird could become a Celtic due to the latter's collegiate standing, Auerbach sensed that Bird was the man to rejuvenate the proud organization. Five other teams had a shot at Bird, but all passed.

In 1981, Boston was again the home of the NBA championship trophy but not before Auerbach orchestrated another blockbuster trade, as he dealt the first pick in the 1981 draft to Golden State for Robert Parish and the third overall pick (Kevin McHale). The master had struck again, as Boston added titles in 1984 and 1986 with the keen additions of Danny Ainge and Dennis Johnson among others.

Auerbach has been the recipient of numerous distinguished awards and honors throughout his career. In 1968, he was enshrined in the Basketball Hall of Fame in Springfield, Massachusetts for his coaching successes. When the NBA chose its Silver Anniversary Team honoring the best of the league's first 25 years, Red was chosen as coach of that distinguished team. In 1982, he was elected to the Washington Hall of Stars, a Hall of Fame which involved people from all sports. Red was also honored as NBA Coach of the Year in 1965, a trophy that now bears his name, and NBA Executive of the Year in 1980. Also, in that year, he was selected to the NBA's 35th Anniversary Team as "Greatest Coach in the History of the NBA," by the PBWAA.

In 1985, The Red Auerbach Fund, the establishment of a

Red with Chief

fund in the great coach's name, was created to promote athletic, recreational and other youth development activities in Boston and throughout the Commonwealth of Massachusetts. January 4, 1985 will always be a special day in Red's heart and in Boston sports history as the Celtics' family saluted its patriarch by having the number "2" retired in his honor (emblematic as the second most important person in the organization's annals, after founder Walter Brown). Nine months later, on September 20, 1985 (Red's 68th birthday), a life-size sculpture of Auerbach was unveiled and placed in Boston's notorious Faneuil Hall Marketplace so the public would have a lasting tribute to this basketball genius and legend.

He has received six honorary degrees from various institutions. Red values such honors so much that he kept a previous commitment to American International College by delivering their commencement speech although it required him to be a no-show in the Boston Garden for the deciding game in the Celtics-Hawks best-of-seven thriller on May 22,

1988. AIC presented Auerbach with a Doctor of Humanities Honorary Degree. A week earlier, on May 15, he received a Doctor of Arts Honorary Degree from Stonehill College. He has also received the Honorary Doctorate Degree in Humane Letters from Franklin Pierce College on May 24, 1981, the University of Massachusetts (Boston) in 1982, and from Boston University on May 13, 1984. In 1986, Central New England College honored him with an Honorary Doctorate Degree in Business Administration.

Red is the author of five books. His first, *Basketball for the Player, the Fan and Coach*, has been translated into seven languages and is the largest-selling basketball book in print. His second book, *Winning the Hard Way*, was co-authored with Paul Sann. Then came the first of two publications written in conjunction with Joe Fitzgerald, *Red Auerbach: An Autobiography.* The more recent publication is *Red Auerbach On and Off the Court.* In October, 1991, Auerbach's latest book, *M.B.A.: Management by Auerbach,* was co-authored with Ken Dooley. In 1987, an excellent instructional video entitled *Winning Basketball* became available to the public featuring the insight, thoughts and philosophy of Red and three-time NBA Most Valuable Player and Celtics' captain Larry Bird.

Auerbach has frequently been recognized for his many accomplishments in the world of basketball. But just as deserved is his recognition as one of the great organizational leaders in corporate America.

Born in Brooklyn, New York, Red attended Eastern District High School in that city, and attended Seth Low Junior College in New York and George Washington University in the District of Columbia. He played three years of college basketball at GW, and was the team's leading scorer and defensive specialist.

Red (9/20/17) and his wife Dorothy live in Washington, D.C. The couple, married since 1941, are the proud parents of two daughters: Nancy, who is the deputy postmaster in the House of Representatives and is married to CNN anchorman Reid Collins; and Randy, who is Vice-President of Creative Affairs for Mel Brooks' Films in Hollywood. Red and Dorothy have one granddaughter, Julie, who is a student at GW and was recently married to Eric Fleiger.

Red

DAVE GAVITT

SENIOR EXECUTIVE VICE PRESIDENT

In the two years that Dave Gavitt has governed the Boston Celtics, a rebirth of enthusiasm has embraced the entire organization. Through his assemblance of a dedicated and discerning basketball operations staff, a strong collection of young individuals grace the parquet floor through the recent drafts of college personnel.

This is precisely the reason when the NBA's premier corporation sought a new man to regulate the organization after its sudden failure in the 1990 Playoffs, Gavitt was the solitary choice. Citations of excellence came from players to front office types to the Commissioner of the National Basketball Association, David Stern, who elucidated: "I've worked a lot with Dave, and I think he's got terrific basketball expertise. He's also a terrific person. He really cares about the game. Dave's been great for the game. I couldn't be happier for the Celtics, Dave, or the NBA." The definitive New Englander, Gavitt is a native of Westerly, Rhode Island. He was raised in Peterborough, New Hampshire, and graduated from Peterborough High School in 1955. Four years later, he graduated from Dartmouth College where he received a diploma in History, and three varsity basketball and baseball letters.

From there, Gavitt became the possessor of an impressive administrative resumé. Commencing in 1960 at Worcester (Mass.) Academy as the Assistant Basketball Coach and Baseball Coach, Gavitt continued with stops at Providence College (1962-66) as Assistant Basketball Coach and Tennis Coach, and Dartmouth College as Assistant Basketball Coach (for half of 1966-67, Head Coach for the remainder of the same season through 1968-69, where he compiled an 18-33 record); then came the site where his prominence was strengthened, Providence College.

From 1969-79, as the Friar's sideline leader (he was also the school's Director of Athletics from 1971-82), his teams were a combined 227-117, including the 1972-73 squad which advanced Cinderella-like to the NCAA Final Four. He was voted New England Coach of the Year in 1968, 1971, 1972, 1973, and 1977. A splendid opportunity was bestowed on Gavitt when he was duly chosen Head Coach of the 1980 US Olympic basketball team.

But the most pivotal moment of his amateur career came as the Big East Conference Commissioner. As its originator, Gavitt built the Big East Conference from a fledgling league in 1979 to a superior group of athletic institutions. Eight times, Big East

schools represented the NCAA Final Four in Gavitt's tenure; those squads advanced to the championship title game six times, including victories in 1984 by Georgetown and 1985 by Villanova. Gavitt was responsible for a conference that evolved into one of the most prosperous and puissant during his direction. He negotiated television contracts peerlessly, evidenced by the continuous upward gross income throughout the league's existence.

Gavitt, as President of USA Basketball, constructed arguably the greatest team in the sport's history as the 1992 US Olympians proudly represented the country in Barcelona, Spain. He was a member of the NCAA Basketball Tournament Committee from 1978-84, a committee he chaired from 1981-84. Gavitt also chaired that committee during the period of growth to a 64-team field, while also introducing the usage of domed stadiums to the Final Four. He has been the recipient of honorary degrees from Franklin Pierce, Providence College, and St. John's University.

May 30, 1990 marked the dawning of a new era for the dynasty-laden Celtics, as Gavitt took the reins of the club's future. A man who exudes personna grata, Gavitt's marvelous reputation has no boundaries whether on the personal or professional level.

Dave (10/26/37), and his wife, the former Julie Garraghan (a 1964 graduate of Skidmore College, who originates from Kingston, NY), have two sons, Dan (26, a 1988 Dartmouth graduate), and Corey (25, a 1989 graduate of the University of North Carolina).

Gavitt speaks with Alan Cohen.

JAN VOLK

GENERAL MANAGER

No one affiliated with the Boston Celtics' organization, past or present, has risen through the ranks as substantially as Jan Volk, a member of the staff for the past 21 years. In that time, he has progressed through a variety of behind-the-scenes activities to his current role of Executive Vice-President and General Manager. Since being appointed to this position in 1984, Volk has been an instrumental figure in molding teams which have compiled a 447-209 (.681) regular season record, six Atlantic Division titles, three Eastern Conference crowns, and one NBA Championship, in 1986. The 1986 team was arguably the finest professional basketball team of this era.

He has made many player transactions that have strengthened the Celtics, and in some cases those moves have led to confounding reactions from baffled rivals. Volk is accountable for the acquisitions, contractual negotiations, renegotiations, and ultimate signings of all current Celtics' players. He maintains a well-deserved reputation as a foremost authority on the NBA salary cap, a unique system of checks and balances designed to manage the escalating costs of players salaries in an attempt to limit the expenditures of operating a league franchise.

A native of Davenport, Iowa, Volk grew up in Newton, Massachusetts and spent his summers as a youth working at his father's summer camp in Marshfield, where Red Auerbach held the Celtics' rookie camp for over twenty years. He attended Newton North High School, graduated from Colby College in 1968 and received his Law Degree from Columbia University in 1971. After passing the Massachusetts Bar Exam in June of 1971, he began his full-time employment with the Celtics.

Starting as Director of Ticket Sales, Volk gradually broadened his areas of responsibility and experience. He took over the team's equipment purchases and travel arrangements, before becoming Business Manager. Slowly, he began to convince Auerbach that his legal expertise could be utilized in the negotiating and drafting of player contracts. In 1974, Volk became the team's Legal Counsel and in 1976 he was named Vice-President of the club. In 1981, he assumed the additional responsibilities of Assistant General Manager, before the promotion to his existing post on July 11, 1984.

Jan, his wife Lissa, and their two children, Shari (15) and Matthew (10), live in Wayland, Massachusetts. He approaches his various hobbies — furniture-building, photography, and US and European history — with the same intensity as his management of the Celtics.

Gavitt and Volk confer.

CHRIS FORD

HEAD COACH

A prerequisite to any coach's success is to get the most out of his players and Chris Ford accomplished that by overcoming debilitating injuries to propel the Boston Celtics to their second straight Atlantic Division title. During his marvelous rookie season performance, he joined Ed Macauley, Billy Cunningham, and Pat Riley as the fourth rookie Head Coach in the All-Star Game; thus, Ford became the third Head Coach in Celtics' history to win division titles in his first two years.

A member of the Celtics' family since 1978, Chris attained a reputation of intelligence, leadership, and spirited involvement as a player in each game, characteristics which led to the June 12, 1990 announcement of his first ever head coaching assignment.

Drafted in the second-round (the 17th pick overall by Detroit in 1972), after a distinguished collegiate career at Villanova (he was elected to the Wildcats' Hall of Fame in 1988), Chris spent his first six years in the NBA with the Pistons. A valuable contributor for the Motor City squad, his steal of an inbounds pass and eventual game-winning basket in Game Three of the Pistons-Bucks mini-series on April 17, 1976 was once considered the top play in the club's history.

In the early stages of his seventh season in Motown, Ford was dealt to Boston with a second-round draft pick (Tracy Jackson) for Earl Tatum on October 18, 1978; he was voted the team's Most Valuable Player that season. On October 12, 1979 as Boston hosted Houston, Ford converted the NBA's initial three-point field goal in the first year of the trifecta. He developed a reputation as one of the league's best three-point bombers, finishing second that season to Seattle's Fred Brown. Ford also became the fifth player to connect on a four-point play when he completed the feat on November 22, 1980 vs. Cleveland. He became Nate Archibald's backcourt partner throughout the Celtics' successful 1981 championship drive, then retired after 1981-82.

Christopher Joseph Ford played ten years in the NBA, appeared in 794 regular season games, averaged 9.2 points, and made 37.5% (126-for-336) of his three-point field goals. He saw action in 58 playoff encounters and averaged 7.5 points.

In between his playing and coaching stints with the Celtics, Ford joined the Celtics' radio announcing crew and did some volunteer coaching with the Boston College basketball program. Upon the completion of the BC season, Chris was offered a job at that school as an Assistant Coach to Gary Williams; however, Ford rejoined the Celtics on June 9, 1983 when K.C. Jones and Red Auerbach offered him a similar position.

Ford engaged in two world championships within his first three years on the bench. He entered an elite group of Celtics' personnel (Bill Russell, Tom Heinsohn, and Jones) who have earned championship rings as both a player and coach.

Chris (1/11/49), his wife Kathy, and their four children, Chris (6/25/75), Katie (4/12/78), Anthony (5/13/82), and Michael (12/6/84) live in Lynnfield, Massachusetts during the season. The family makes Margate, New Jersey their home during the summer months.

Ford at work

DON CASEY

ASSISTANT COACH

Don Casey is a man with an extensive coaching resumé who commands tremendous respect around the NBA circuit. Entering his third season with the Celtics, Casey accepted Chris Ford's offer in the summer of 1990 to complete the team's coaching staff.

Casey was the Head Coach at Temple University from 1973-74 through 1981-82, where he compiled an impressive record of 151-94 (.616). The Owls finished first or second in the East Coast Conference in his last seven years, and he posted 20 or more wins three times. He was twice voted East Coast Conference Coach of the Year and he led Temple to one NCAA postseason tournament and three NIT berths.

In 1982-83, Casey joined the NBA ranks as an Assistant Coach to Paul Westhead (Chicago Bulls), then became an assistant to Jim Lynam (Los Angeles Clippers) the following campaign. In 1984-85, Casey was a Head Coach in the Italian Professional League, then returned to the NBA's Clippers as an assistant under Don Chaney and Gene Shue for the next three-plus seasons.

On January 19, 1989, Casey became the Clippers' Head Coach replacing Shue for the remainder of that season. Casey was subsequently signed for the 1989-90 season as the Clippers' top man on July 13, 1989, and continued in that capacity throughout the season. The Clippers finished at 30-52, sixth place in the Pacific Division, and were 41-85 under his direction.

Casey has developed a reputation in coaching against zone defenses, and has authored a book on the subject entitled *Temple of Zones*.

The affable Casey was born in Collingswood, New Jersey, attended high school at Catholic High in Camden, NJ, and graduated from Temple University in 1960 (did not play collegiate basketball).

Magnificently dedicated to proper physical conditioning, Casey is such a fervent runner that he was a feature subject of *Runner's World* magazine in the Fall of 1992, and is a main client of Reebok International. Casey also has been known to enjoy a cup of espresso or cappucino on occasion.

Don (6/17/37), and his wife Dwynne, have three children, Lee Ann (25), Michael (23), and Sean (21). During the off-season, the couple maintains a home in California, while living in Boston during the season.

JON JENNINGS

ASSISTANT COACH

When Chris Ford was appointed Head Coach of the Boston Celtics, one of his first tasks was the completion of his coaching staff. Without wavering, Ford selected Jon Jennings, who in addition to his obligations as an Assistant Coach, also administers the scouting schedule for collegiate, professional and foreign talent.

Jennings, a native of Richmond, Indiana, has an impressive resumé of basketball experience. While attending Indiana University from 1981-85, Jennings served Head Coach Bob Knight in various roles during his sophomore and junior years.

In 1983, Jennings served as a summer intern with the Indiana Pacers. His duties included ticket sales, public relations, and assisting George Irvine, the club's Vice-President of Basketball Operations. Jennings acquired valuable knowledge in that last capacity coordinating all college, CBA, and NBA scouting. At the age of 20, Jennings was hired by Irvine, who brought him to Los Angeles to assist in coaching duties with the Pacers' summer league squad.

Upon Irvine's appointment to Indiana's head coaching position, Jennings began to scout and coordinate videos fulltime. Jennings had a bird's-eye view of Pacers' home games, and upon the completion of first-half action, would edit a two-minute tape used in the halftime discussion between players and coaches.

Jennings joined the NBA Champion Boston Celtics in the summer of 1986, working as the club's initial Video Coordinator. When Jim Rodgers was chosen the leader of the Green, Jennings responsibilities increased as he scouted Boston's future opponents as well as college players. Jon also assumed the duties of keeping statistical charts, breaking down the opponents' offensive and defensive patterns and formulating this information into game plans.

Jon (10/2/62) is single and lives in Watertown, MA. A devotee of Winston Churchill, Jennings lists his interests as history, politics, reading and painting.

Sam Jones

RECORDS

CELTICS IN NAISMITH MEMORIAL BASKETBALL HALL OF FAME
at Springfield, Massachusetts

IN ORDER OF ELECTION:
Ed Macauley (1960)
Andy Phillip (1961)
John (Honey) Russell (1964)
Walter Brown (1965)
Bill Mokray (1965)
Alvin (Doggie) Julian (1967)
Arnold (Red) Auerbach (1968)
Bob Cousy (1970)
Bill Russell (1974)
Bill Sharman (1975)
Frank Ramsey (1981)
John Havlicek (1983)
Sam Jones (1983)
Tom Heinsohn (1985)
Bob Houbregs (1986)
Pete Maravich (1986)
Clyde Lovellette (1987)
K.C. Jones (1988)
Dave Bing (1989)
Pete Maravich (1989)
Dave Cowens (1991)
Nate (Tiny) Archibald (1991)

RETIRED CELTICS NUMBERS

1 — Walter Brown
2 — Arnold (Red) Auerbach
6 — Bill Russell
10 — Jo Jo White
14 — Bob Cousy
15 — Tom Heinsohn
16 — Tom (Satch) Sanders
17 — John Havlicek
18 — Dave Cowens
      Jim Loscutoff*
19 — Don Nelson
21 — Bill Sharman
22 — Ed Macauley
23 — Frank Ramsey
24 — Sam Jones
25 — K.C. Jones

* Loscutoff's jersey was retired, but number 18 was kept active for Dave Cowens.

CELTICS ON ALL-NBA TEAM
(Selected by the media)

Player	1st Team	2nd Team	3rd Team	Total
Bob Cousy	10	2	0	12
John Havlicek	4	7	0	11
Bill Russell	3	8	0	11
Larry Bird	9	1	0	10
Bill Sharman	4	3	0	7
Ed Macauley	3	1	0	4
Tom Heinsohn	0	4	0	4
Dave Cowens	0	3	0	3
Sam Jones	0	3	0	3
Jo Jo White	0	2	0	2
Kevin McHale	1	0	0	1
Ed Sadowski	1	0	0	1
Nate Archibald	0	1	0	1
Robert Parish	0	1	2	3

INDIVIDUAL AWARDS

NBA EXECUTIVE OF THE YEAR
(Originated in 1972-73; selected by The Sporting News)
1979-80 Red Auerbach

NBA COACH OF THE YEAR
(Originated in 1962-63; selected by the media)
1964-65 Red Auerbach
1972-73 Tom Heinsohn
1979-80 Bill Fitch

NBA MOST VALUABLE PLAYER
(Originated in 1955-56; selected by NBA players)

1956-57	Bob Cousy
1957-58	Bill Russell
1960-61	Bill Russell
1961-62	Bill Russell
1962-63	Bill Russell
1964-65	Bill Russell
1972-73	Dave Cowens
1983-84	Larry Bird
1984-85	Larry Bird
1985-86	Larry Bird

PLAYOFFS' MOST VALUABLE PLAYER
(Originated in 1969; selected by Sport magazine)

1974	John Havlicek
1976	Jo Jo White
1981	Cedric Maxwell
1984	Larry Bird
1986	Larry Bird

CELTICS ON NBA'S 35TH ANNIVERSARY TEAM

(Chosen in 1980 to honor the top performers in the league's first 35 seasons.)

Coach: Arnold (Red) Auerbach

Players: Bob Cousy
           John Havlicek
           Bill Russell*

* Russell voted the league's greatest all-time player. (In all 11 players were chosen. The other eight: Kareem Abdul-Jabbar, Elgin Baylor, Wilt Chamberlain, Julius Erving, George Mikan, Bob Pettit, Oscar Robertson and Jerry West.)

CELTICS ON NBA'S SILVER ANNIVERSARY TEAM

(Chosen in 1971 to honor the top performers in the league's first 25 seasons.)

Coach: Arnold (Red) Auerbach

Players: Bob Cousy
           Bill Russell
           Bill Sharman
           Sam Jones

(In all 10 players were chosen. The other six: George Mikan, Bob Pettit, Dolph Schayes, Paul Arizin, Bob Davies and Joe Fulks.)

NBA ROOKIE OF THE YEAR

(Originated in 1952-53; selected by the media)

1956-57 Tom Heinsohn
1970-71 Dave Cowens
   (shared with Portland's Geoff Petrie)
1979-80 Larry Bird

NBA ALL-DEFENSIVE TEAM

(Originated in 1968-69; selected by the coaches)

1968-69	Bill Russell (1st team)
	John Havlicek (2nd team)
	Tom Sanders (2nd team)
1969-70	John Havlicek (2nd team)
1970-71	John Havlicek (2nd team)
1971-72	John Havlicek (1st team)
	Don Chaney (2nd team)
1972-73	John Havlicek (1st team)
	Don Chaney (2nd team)
	Paul Silas (2nd team)
1973-74	John Havlicek (1st team)
	Don Chaney (2nd team)
1974-75	John Havlicek (1st team)
	Paul Silas (1st team)
	Don Chaney (2nd team)
	Dave Cowens (2nd team)
1975-76	Dave Cowens (1st team)
	John Havlicek (1st team)
	Paul Silas (1st team)
1979-80	Dave Cowens (2nd team)
1981-82	Larry Bird (2nd team)
1982-83	Larry Bird (2nd team)
	Kevin McHale (2nd team)
1983-84	Larry Bird (2nd team)
	Dennis Johnson (2nd team)
1984-85	Dennis Johnson (2nd team)
1985-86	Kevin McHale (1st team)
	Dennis Johnson (2nd team)
1986-87	Kevin McHale (1st team)
	Dennis Johnson (1st team)
1987-88	Kevin McHale (1st team)
1988-89	Kevin McHale (2nd team)
1989-90	Kevin McHale (2nd team)

NBA SIXTH MAN

(Originated in 1982-83; selected by the media)

1983-84   Kevin McHale
1984-85   Kevin McHale
1985-86   Bill Walton

NBA ALL-ROOKIE TEAM

(Originated in 1962-63; selected by the coaches)

1962-63   John Havlicek
1969-70   Jo Jo White
1970-71   Dave Cowens
1979-80   Larry Bird
1980-81   Kevin McHale
1988-89   Brian Shaw (2nd team)
1990-91   Dee Brown

McHale won the Sixth Man Award for two seasons.

BOSTON CELTICS' COACHES

Year	Coach	Regular Season		Playoffs	
		Won	Lost	Won	Lost
1946-47	John (Honey) Russell	22	38	—	—
1947-48	John (Honey) Russell	20	28	1	2
1948-49	Alvin (Doggy) Julian	25	35	—	—
1949-50	Alvin (Doggy) Julian	22	46	—	—
1950-51	Arnold (Red) Auerbach	39	30	0	2
1951-52	Arnold (Red) Auerbach	39	27	1	2
1952-53	Arnold (Red) Auerbach	46	25	3	3
1953-54	Arnold (Red) Auerbach	42	30	2	4
1954-55	Arnold (Red) Auerbach	36	36	3	4
1955-56	Arnold (Red) Auerbach	39	33	1	2
*1956-57	Arnold (Red) Auerbach	44	28	7	3
1957-58	Arnold (Red) Auerbach	49	23	6	5
*1958-59	Arnold (Red) Auerbach	52	20	8	3
*1959-60	Arnold (Red) Auerbach	59	16	5	
*1960-61	Arnold (Red) Auerbach	57	22	8	2
*1961-62	Arnold (Red) Auerbach	60	20	8	6
*1962-63	Arnold (Red) Auerbach	58	22	8	5
*1963-64	Arnold (Red) Auerbach	59	21	8	2
*1964-65	Arnold (Red) Auerbach	62	18	8	4
*1965-66	Arnold (Red) Auerbach	54	26	11	6
1966-67	Bill Russell	60	21	4	5
*1967-68	Bill Russell	54	28	12	7
*1968-69	Bill Russell	48	34	12	6
1969-70	Tom Heinsohn	34	48	—	—
1970-71	Tom Heinsohn	44	38	—	—
1971-72	Tom Heinsohn	56	26	5	6
1972-73	Tom Heinsohn	68	14	7	6
*1973-74	Tom Heinsohn	56	26	12	6
1974-75	Tom Heinsohn	60	22	6	5
*1975-76	Tom Heinsohn	54	28	12	6
1976-77	Tom Heinsohn	44	38	5	4
1977-78	Tom Heinsohn	11	23		
	Thomas (Satch) Sanders	21	27	—	—
1978-79	Thomas (Satch) Sanders	2	12		
	Dave Cowens	27	41	—	—
1979-80	Bill Fitch	61	21	5	4
*1980-81	Bill Fitch	62	20	12	5
1981-82	Bill Fitch	63	19	7	5
1982-83	Bill Fitch	56	26	2	5
*1983-84	K.C. Jones	62	20	15	8
1984-85	K.C. Jones	63	19	13	8
*1985-86	K.C. Jones	67	15	15	3
1986-87	K.C. Jones	59	23	13	10
1987-88	K.C. Jones	57	25	9	—
1988-89	Jimmy Rodgers	42	40	0	3
1989-90	Jimmy Rodgers	52	30	2	3
1990-91	Chris Ford	56	26	5	7
TOTALS	Eleven Coaches	2223	1254	264	180

*NBA Championships

COACHING RECORDS

(Boston only)

Coach	Regular Season Record	Playoff Record
John Russell	42-66 (.389)	1-2 (.333)
Alvin Julian	47-81 (.367)	0-0 (.000)
Red Auerbach	795-397 (.667)	90-58 (.608)
Bill Russell	162-83 (.661)	28-18 (.609)
Tom Heinsohn	427-263 (.619)	47-33 (.588)
Tom Sanders	23-39 (.371)	0-0 (.000)
Dave Cowens	27-41 (.397)	0-0 (.000)
Bill Fitch	242-86 (.738)	26-19 (.578)
K.C. Jones	308-102 (.751)	65-37 (.637)
Jim Rodgers	94-70 (.573)	2-6 (.250)
Chris Ford	56-26 (.683)	5-7 (.417)
TOTALS	2223-1254 (.639)	264-180 (.595)

CELTICS' OWNERSHIP

1946-1948:	Walter Brown/Boston Garden-Arena Corporation
1948-1950:	Walter Brown
1950-1964:	Walter Brown/Lou Pieri
1964-1965:	Lou Pieri/Marjorie Brown
1965-1968:	Marvin Kratter/National Equities
1968-1969:	Ballantine Brewery
1969-1971:	E. E. (Woody) Erdman/Trans-National Comm.
1971-1972:	Investors' Funding Corporation
1972-1974:	Bob Schmertz/Leisure Technology
1974-1975:	Bob Schmertz/Irv Levin
1975-1978:	Irv Levin
1978-1979:	John Y. Brown/Harry Mangurian Jr.
1979-1983:	Harry Mangurian Jr.
1983-present:	Don Gaston, Paul Dupee, Jr., Alan Cohen

CELTICS' ASSISTANT COACHES

1946-47-1947-48:	Danny Silva
1948-49-1949-50:	Henry McCarthy
1949-50:	Art Spector
1972-73-1976-77:	John Killilea
1977-78:	Tom (Satch) Sanders
1978-79:	Bob MacKinnon
1977-78-1982-83:	K.C. Jones
1980-81-1987-88:	Jimmy Rodgers
1983-84-1989-90:	Chris Ford
1984-85-1987-88:	Ed Badger
1988-89-1989-90:	Lanny Van Eman
1990-91-present	Don Casey
1990-91-present	Jon P. Jennings

CELTICS' TRAINERS

1946-47-1957-58:	Harvey Cohn
1958-59-1966-67:	Edward (Buddy) LeRoux
1967-68-1970-71:	Joe DeLauri
1971-72-1978-79:	Frank Challant
1979-80-1986-87:	Ray Melchiorre
1987-88-present:	Ed Lacerte

Scout Forddy Anderson.

Alan Cohen.

Parish heads into his 17th NBA season.

110

CELTICS' CAREER LEADERS - REGULAR SEASON

GAMES

1. John Havlicek — 1,270
2. Bill Russell — 963
3. Robert Parish — 953
4. Bob Cousy — 917
5. Tom Sanders — 916
6. Don Nelson — 872
7. Sam Jones — 871
8. Kevin McHale — 900
9. Larry Bird — 897
10. Dave Cowens — 726

MINUTES

1. John Havlicek — 46,471
2. Bill Russell — 40,726
3. Larry Bird — 34,430
4. Robert Parish — 30,845
5. Bob Cousy — 30,131
6. Dave Cowens — 28,551
7. Kevin Mchale — 28,444
8. Jo Jo White — 26,770
9. Tom Sanders — 22,164
10. Bill Sharman — 21,793

POINTS

1. John Havlicek — 26,395
2. Larry Bird — 21,791
3. Bob Cousy — 16,955
4. Kevin McHale — 16,573
5. Sam Jones — 15,411
6. Bill Russell — 14,522
7. Robert Parish — 13,985
8. Dave Cowens — 13,192
9. Jo Jo White — 13,985
10. Bill Sharman — 12,287

AVERAGE POINTS (3 Yrs. Min.)

1. Larry Bird — 24.3
2. John Havlicek — 20.8
3. Ed Macauley — 18.9
4. Tom Heinsohn — 18.6
5. Bob Cousy — 18.5
6. Kevin McHale — 18.4
7. Jo Jo White — 18.3
8. Dave Cowens — 18.2
9. Bill Sharman — 18.1
10. Bailey Howell — 18.0

FIELD GOALS ATTEMPTED

1. John Havlicek — 23,930
2. Larry Bird — 16,576
3. Bob Cousy — 16,465
4. Sam Jones — 13,745
5. Bill Russell — 12,930
6. Jo Jo White — 12,782
7. Dave Cowens — 12,193
8. Robert Parish — 12,056
9. Tom Heinshn — 11,787
10. Kevin McHale — 11,685

FREE THROWS ATTEMPTED

1. John Havlicek — 6,589
2. Bob Cousy — 5,753
3. Bill Russell — 5,614
4. Larry Bird — 4,531
5. Kevin McHale — 4,359
6. Robert Parish — 4,048
7. Sam Jones — 3,572
8. Ed Macauley — 3,518
9. Cedric Maxwell — 3,496
10. Bill Sharman — 3,451

FREE THROWS MADE

1. John Havlicek — 5,369
2. Bob Cousy — 4,621
3. Larry Bird — 3,810
4. Kevin McHale — 3,960
5. Bill Russell — 3,148
6. Bill Sharman — 3,047
7. Robert Parish — 2,963
8. Sam Jones — 2,869
9. Cedric Maxwell — 2,738
10. Ed Macauley — 2,724

FREE THROW PERCENTAGE (1,500 Att.)

1. Larry Bird — .886 (3,960-4,471)
2. Bill Sharman — .883(3,047-3,451)
3. Larry Siegfried — .855 (1,500-1,755)
4. Jo Jo White — .833 (1,892-2,270)
5. John Havlicek — .815 (5,369-6,589)
6. Frank Ramsey — .804 (2,480-3,083)
7. Bob Cousy — .803 (4,621-5,753)
8. Sam Jones — .803 (2,869-3,572)
9. Kevin McHale — .796(3,470-4,359)
10. Nate Archibald — .790 (1,401-1,773)

ASSISTS

1. Bob Cousy — 6,945
2. John Havlicek — 6,114
3. Larry Bird — 5,695
4. Bill Russell — 4,100
5. Jo Jo White — 3,686
6. Dennis Johnson — 3,001
7. K.C. Jones — 2,904
8. Dave Cowens — 2,828
9. Nate Archibald — 2,563
10. Sam Jones — 2,209

REBOUNDS

1. Bill Russell — 21,620
2. Dave Cowens — 10,170
3. Robert Parish — 9,769
4. Larry Bird — 8,974
5. John Havlicek — 8,007
6. Kevin McHale — 6,764
7. Tom Sanders — 5,798
8. Tom Heinsohn — 5,749
9. Bob Cousy — 4,781
10. Don Nelson — 4,517

FIELD GOALS MADE

1. John Havlicek — 10,513
2. Larry Bird — 8,591
3. Sam Jones — 6,271
4. Kevin McHale — 6,532
5. Robert Parish — 6,711
6. Bob Cousy — 6,167
7. Bill Russell — 5,687
8. Jo Jo White — 5,648
9. Dave Cowens — 5,608
10. Tom Heinsohn — 4,773

FIELD GOAL PERCENTAGE (2,000 ATT.)

1. Kevin McHale — .559 (6,532-11,685)
2. Cedric Maxwell — .559 (2,786-4,984)
3. Robert Parish — .567 (6,711-12,056)
4. Rick Robey — .510 (1,144-2,241)
5. Larry Bird — .496 (8,591-17,334)
6. Danny Ainge — .490 (2,266-4,621)
7. Gerald Henderson — .489 (1,467-3,002)
8. Don Nelson — .484 (3,717-7,672)
9. Bailey Howell — .480 (2,290-4,766)
10. Nate Archibald — .469 (1,567-3,338)

PERSONAL FOULS

1. John Havlicek — 3,281
2. Tom Sanders — 3,044
3. Dave Cowens — 2,783
4. Robert Parish — 2,734
5. Kevin McHale — 2,632
6. Bill Russell — 2,592
7. Tom Heisnohn — 2,454
8. Bob Cousy — 2,231
9. Larry Bird — 2,197
10. Frank Ramsey — 2,158

DISQUALIFICATIONS

1. Tom Sanders — 94
2. Frank Ramsey — 87
3. Dave Cowens — 86
4. Tom Heisnohn — 58
5. Robert Parish — 47
6. Bob Brannum — 42
7. Don Chaney — 40
8. Jim Loscutoff — 40
9. Cedric Maxwell — 32

CELTICS' INDIVIDUAL REGULAR-SEASON RECORDS

SCORING

60	Larry Bird vs Atlanta (at New Orleans)	March 12, 1985
56	Kevin McHale vs Detroit	March 3, 1985
53	Larry Bird vs Indiana	March 30, 1983
51	Sam Jones at Detroit	October 29, 1965
50	Larry Bird at Dallas	March 10, 1986
50	Larry Bird vs Atlanta	November 10, 1989
49	Larry Bird vs Washington	January 27, 1988
49	Larry Bird at Phoenix	February 15, 1988
49	Larry Bird vs Portland	March 15, 1992
48	Larry Bird vs Houston	March 17, 1985
48	Larry Bird vs Portland	January 27, 1985
48	Larry Bird vs Atlanta	December 9, 1984
47	Larry Bird vs New York	April 12, 1987
47	Larry Bird at Portland	February 14, 1986
47	Larry Bird vs Detroit	November 27, 1985
47	Larry Bird vs Milwaukee	April 12, 1985

FIELD GOALS MADE

22	Larry Bird vs New York	April 12, 1987
22	Larry Bird vs Atlanta (at New Orleans)	March 12, 1985
22	Kevin McHale vs Detroit	March 3, 1985
21	Larry Bird at Portland	February 14, 1986
21	Larry Bird vs Indiana	March 30, 1983
21	Sam Jones at Detroit	October 29, 1965
20	Larry Bird vs Atlanta	December 9, 1984
20	Larry Bird vs Washington	January 27, 1988
20	Danny Ainge vs Phoenix	December 9, 1988

FREE THROWS MADE

20	Nate Archibald vs Chicago	January 16, 1980
19	Cedric Maxwell vs New Jersey	January 14, 1979
19	John Havlicek vs Seattle	February 6, 1970
19	Frank Ramsey at Detroit	December 3, 1957
19	Bill Sharman at Philadelphia	March 8, 1956

ASSISTS

28	Bob Cousy vs Minneapolis	February 27, 1959
23	Nate Archibald vs Denver	February 5, 1982
21	Bob Cousy vs St Louis	December 21, 1960
19	Nate Archibald at San Antonio	October 23, 1979
19	Bob Cousy vs Cincinnati	February 19, 1963
19	Bob Cousy vs Syracuse	November 24, 1956
18	Nate Archibald at Seattle	December 16, 1982
18	Bob Cousy at New York	November 21, 1959
18	Bob Cousy vs New York	January 18, 1953

REBOUNDS

51	Bill Russell vs Syracuse	February 5, 1960
49	Bill Russell vs Philadelphia	November 16, 1957
49	Bill Russell vs Detroit	March 11, 1965
43	Bill Russell vs Los Angeles	January 20, 1963
41	Bill Russell vs Syracuse	February 12, 1958
41	Bill Russell vs San Francisco	March 14, 1965
40	Bill Russell vs Cincinnati	December 12, 1958
40	Bill Russell vs Philadelphia	February 12, 1961

OPPONENTS' INDIVIDUAL REGULAR SEASON RECORDS

SCORING

64	Elgin Baylor, at Minneapolis	November 8, 1959
62	Wilt Chamberlain, Philadelphia at Boston	January 14, 1962
55	Kareem Abdul-Jabbar, at Milwaukee	December 10, 1971
54	Dominique Wilkins, at Atlanta	February 3, 1987

FIELD GOALS MADE

27	Wilt Chamberlain, Philadelphia at Boston	January 14, 1962
25	Elgin Baylor, at Minneapolis	November 8, 1959
25	Wilt Chamberlain, Phil vs Boston at NY	February 23, 1960

FREE THROWS MADE

22	Richie Guerin, New York at Boston	February 11, 1961
20	Kareem Abdul-Jabbar, Milwaukee at Boston	March 8, 1970

ASSISTS

25	Kevin Porter, at Detroit	March 9, 1979
21	Clem Haskins, Chicago at Boston (OT)	December 6, 1969
21	Earvin Johnson, Lakers at Boston	December 15, 1989

REBOUNDS

55	Wilt Chamberlain, at Philadelphia	November 24, 1960
43	Wilt Chamberlain, at Philadelphia	March 6, 1965
42	Wilt Chamberlain, at Philadelphia	January 15, 1960
42	Wilt Chamberlain, at Philadelphia	January 14, 1966
42	Wilt Chamberlain, at Los Angeles	March 7, 1969

Cousy

Larry owns his share of records.

INDIVIDUAL PLAYOFF RECORDS

MOST POINTS

—Game	54	John Havlicek vs. Atlanta	April 1, 1973
—Half	30	Larry Bird vs. Detroit	April 30, 1985
		John Havlicek vs. Atlanta	April 1, 1973
—Quarter	24	Larry Bird vs. Atlanta	May 11, 1988
—Overtime	12	Bob Cousy at Syracuse	March 17, 1954

MOST FIELD GOALS MADE

—Game	24	John Havlicek vs. Atlanta	April 1, 1973
—Half	14	John Havlicek vs. Atlanta	April 1, 1973
—Quarter	10	Larry Bird vs. Atlanta	May 11, 1988

MOST FIELD GOALS ATTEMPTED

—Game	36	John Havlicek vs. Atlanta	April 1, 1973
—Half	21	Larry Bird vs. Detroit	May 8, 1985
—Quarter	13	Dave Cowens vs. Buffalo	March 30, 1974

MOST FREE THROWS MADE

—Game	30	Bob Cousy vs. Syracuse	March 21, 1953
—Half	12	Larry Bird vs. Detroit	April 30, 1985
—Quarter	9	Frank Ramsey vs. Minneapolis	April 4, 1959

MOST FREE THROWS ATTEMPTED

—Game	32	Bob Cousy vs. Syracuse	March 21, 1953
—Half	15	Bill Russell vs. St. Louis	April 11, 1961
—Quarter	10	Frank Ramsey vs. Minneapolis	April 4, 1959

MOST REBOUNDS

—Game	40	Bill Russell vs. Philadelphia	March 23, 1958
		Bill Russell vs. St. Louis	March 29, 1960
		Bill Russell vs. Los Angeles	April 18, 1962
—Half	25	Bill Russell vs. St. Louis	March 29, 1960
		Bill Russell vs. Los Angeles	April 18, 1962
—Quarter	19	Bill Russell vs. Los Angeles	April 18, 1962

MOST ASSISTS

—Game	19	Bob Cousy vs. St. Louis	April 9, 1957
		Bob Cousy at Minneapolis (St. Paul)	April 7, 1959
—Half	11	Larry Bird vs. New York	April 28, 1990
		Dennis Johnson vs. Los Angeles	June 7, 1985
		Bob Cousy vs. Cincinnati	April 10, 1963
		John Havlicek vs. Philadelphia	April 24, 1977
—Quarter	8	Bob Cousy vs. St. Louis	April 9, 1957
		John Havlicek vs. Philadelphia	April 24, 1977

MOST PERSONAL FOULS

—Game	6	Many players	
—Half	6	Gene Conley vs. Syracuse	March 22, 1959
		Frank Ramsey vs. Syracuse	April 1, 1959
—Quarter	5	Greg Kite at Houston	June 1, 1986

MOST CONSECUTIVE FREE THROWS MADE

	56	Bill Sharman	March 18, 1959- April 9, 1959

THREE-POINT FIELD GOALS MADE

—Game	5	Danny Ainge vs. Los Angeles	June 11, 1987
	5	Larry Bird at Milwaukee	May 18, 1986
—Half	5	Danny Ainge vs. Los angeles	June 11, 1987
—Quarter	5	Danny Ainge vs. Los Angeles	June 11, 1987
—Game, no misses	4	Scott Wedman vs. Los Angeles	May 27, 1985

THREE-POINT FIELD GOALS ATTEMPTED

—Game	8	Danny Ainge at Detroit	May 28, 1988

MOST STEALS

—Game	7	Dennis Johnson vs. Atlanta	April 29, 1986

MOST BLOCKS

—Game	7	Robert Parish vs. Philadelphia	May 9, 1982

HIGHEST FIELD GOAL PERCENTAGE

—Game	1.000	Scott Wedman vs. Los Angeles (11-for-11)	May 27, 1985

TEAM PLAYOFF RECORDS

MOST POINTS
—Game	157	vs. New York	April 28, 1990
—Half	83	vs. New York	April 28, 1990
—Quarter	46	vs. St. Louis	March 27, 1960
	46	vs. Detroit	March 24, 1968

MOST FIELD GOALS MADE
—Game	63	vs. New York	April 28, 1990
—Half	34	vs. New York	April 28, 1990
—Quarter	21	vs. Los Angeles	April 18, 1965

MOST FIELD GOALS ATTEMPTED
—Game	140	vs. Syracuse	March 18, 1959
—Half	77	vs. Philadelphia	March 22, 1960
—Quarter	42	vs. Philadelphia	March 22, 1960

MOST FREE THROWS MADE
—Game	57	vs. Syracuse	March 21, 1953
—Half	21	vs. Cleveland	April 25, 1985
—Quarter	15	vs. Cleveland	April 25, 1985

MOST FREE THROWS ATTEMPTED
—Game	64	vs. Syracuse	March 21, 1953
—Half	30	vs. St. Louis	April 9, 1958
—Quarter	18	vs. Los Angeles	April 18, 1962

MOST REBOUNDS
—Game	107	vs. Philadelphia	March 19, 1960
—Half	60	vs. Philadelphia	March 19, 1960
—Quarter	31	vs. Philadelphia	March 19, 1960
		vs. Syracuse	March 23, 1961

MOST ASSISTS
—Game	46	vs. New York	April 28, 1990
—Half	28	vs. New York	April 28, 1990
—Quarter	15	vs. New York	April 28, 1990

MOST PERSONAL FOULS
—Game	52	vs. Syracuse	March 21, 1953
—Half	21	vs. Cincinnati	March 28, 1963
—Quarter	11	vs. Los Angeles	April 17, 1966

MOST DISQUALIFICATIONS
—Game	5	vs. Syracuse	March 21, 1953

MOST CONSECUTIVE WINS
	7	vs. three teams	May 6, 1986- May 29, 1986

MOST CONSECUTIVE LOSSES
	5	vs. Detroit	June 1, 1988- May 2, 1989

THREE-POINT FIELD GOALS MADE
—Game	8	at Milwaukee	May 18, 1986

THREE-POINT FIELD GOALS ATTEMPTED
—Game	12	at Detroit	May 28, 1988
	12	at Milwaukee	May 18, 1986

MOST STEALS
—Game	15	vs. Houston	May 26, 1986
	15	vs. Atlanta	April 29, 1986
	15	vs. New York	May 9, 1984
	15	at LA Lakers	June 6, 1984

MOST BLOCKS
—Game	15	at Washington	May 1, 1982

FEWEST TURNOVERS
—Game	5	vs. Chicago	April 26, 1987

Tom Heinsohn

CELTICS' CAREER PLAYOFFS LEADERS

POINTS

1. Larry Bird	3897
2. John Havlicek	3776
3. Kevin McHale	3106
4. Sam Jones	2909
5. Bill Russell	2673
6. Robert Parish	2495
7. Tom Heinsohn	2058
8. Bob Cousy	2018
9. Dennis Johnson	1733
10. Jo Jo White	1720

AVERAGE POINTS (25 Game Min.)

1. Larry Bird	23.8
2. John Havlicek	22.0
3. Jo Jo White	21.5
4. Tom Heinsohn	19.8
5. Dave Cowens	18.9
6. Sam Jones	18.9
7. Kevin McHale	18.8
8. Bill Sharman	18.5
9. Bob Cousy	18.5
10. Dennis Johnson	16.7

GAMES PLAYED

1. John Havlicek	172
2. Bill Russell	165
3. Kevin McHale	165
4. Larry Bird	164
5. Robert Parish	154
6. Sam Jones	154
7. Don Nelson	134
8. Tom Sanders	130
9. Danny Ainge	112
10. Bob Cousy	109

MINUTES PLAYED

1. Bill Russell	7497
2. John Havlicek	6860
3. Larry Bird	6886
4. Robert Parish	5368
5. Kevin McHale	5603
6. Sam Jones	4654
7. Bob Cousy	4140
8. Dennis Johnson	4096
9. Dave Cowens	3768
10. Jo Jo White	3428

FREE THROWS ATTEMPTED

1. Bill Russell	1106
2. John Havlicek	1012
3. Larry Bird	1008
4. Kevin McHale	958
5. Bob Cousy	799
6. Sam Jones	753
7. Robert Parish	704
8. Tom Heinsohn	568
9. Dennis Johnson	513
10. Frank Ramsey	476

FREE THROWS MADE

1. Larry Bird	901
2. John Havlicek	874
3. Kevin McHale	754
4. Bill Russell	667
5. Bob Cousy	640
6. Sam Jones	611
7. Robert Parish	511
8. Dennis Johnson	429
9. Tom Heinsohn	422
10. Frank Ramsey	393

FREE THROW PERCENTAGE (200 FTM Minimum)

1. Bill Sharman	.911 (370-406)
2. Larry Bird	.890 (901-1102)
3. Dennis Johnson	.836 (429-513)
4. John Havlicek	.836 (874-1046)
5. Larry Siegfried	.834 (256-307)
6. Jo Jo White	.828 (256-309)
7. Frank Ramsey	.826 (393-476)
8. Don Nelson	.819 (385-470)
9. Sam Jones	.811 (611-753)
10. Bob Cousy	.801 (640-799)

ASSISTS

1. Larry Bird	1062
2. Bob Cousy	937
3. John Havlicek	825
4. Bill Russell	770
5. Dennis Johnson	711
6. Danny Ainge	489
7. Jo Jo White	452
8. K.C. Jones	396
9. Sam Jones	358
10. Dave Cowens	333

FIELD GOALS ATTEMPTED

1. John Havlicek	3329
2. Larry Bird	3090
3. Sam Jones	2571
4. Bill Russell	2335
5. Kevin McHale	2090
6. Tom Heinsohn	2035
7. Bob Cousy	2016
8. Robert Parish	1855
9. Jo Jo White	1629
10. Dave Cowens	1627

FIELD GOALS MADE

1. John Havlicek	1451
2. Larry Bird	1458
3. Kevin McHale	1172
4. Sam Jones	1149
5. Bill Russell	1003
6. Robert Parish	992
7. Tom Heinsohn	818
8. Dave Cowens	733
9. Jo Jo White	732
10. Bob Cousy	689

FIELD GOAL PERCENTAGE (200 FGM Minimum)

1. Kevin McHale	.561 (1172-1964)
2. Cedric Maxwell	.546 (356-652)
3. Robert Parish	.503 (934-1858)
4. Don Nelson	.500 (554-1109)
5. Bailey Howell	.498 (306-615)
6. Larry Bird	.472 (1458-3090)
7. Danny Ainge	.465 (479-1030)
8. Gerald Henderson	.454 (244-538)
9. Dave Cowens	.451 (733-1627)
10. Jo Jo White	.449 (732-1629)

REBOUNDS

1. Bill Russell	4104
2. Larry Bird	1683
3. Robert Parish	1514
4. Dave Cowens	1285
5. John Havlicek	1186
6. Kevin McHale	1224
7. Tom Heinsohn	954
8. Tom Sanders	763
9. Paul Silas	763
10. Dennis Johnson	739

PERSONAL FOULS

1. Kevin McHale	565
2. Bill Russell	546
3. Robert Parish	535
4. John Havlicek	517
5. Tom Sanders	508
6. Larry Bird	459
7. Tom Heinsohn	417
8. Dave Cowens	398
9. Sam Jones	395
10. Frank Ramsey	362

DISQUALIFICATIONS

1. Tom Sanders	26
2. Dave Cowens	15
3. Robert Parish	15
4. Charlie Scott	14
5. Tom Heinsohn	14
6. Frank Ramsey	13
7. Bailey Howell	11
8. John Havlicek	9
9. Bob Donham	9
10. Bill Russell	8
11. Jim Loscutoff	8
12. Bob Brannum	8
13. Kevin McHale	8

INDIVIDUAL PLAYOFF PERFORMANCES

Scoring

54	John Havlicek, at Atlanta	April 1, 1973
51	Sam Jones, at New York	March 30, 1967
50	Bob Cousy, vs. Syracuse (4 OT)	March 21, 1953
47	Sam Jones, vs. Cincinnati	April 10, 1963

Field Goals Made

24	John Havlicek, at Atlanta	April 1, 1973
19	Sam Jones, at New York	March 30, 1967

Free Throws Made

30	Bob Cousy, vs. Syracuse (4 OT)	March 21, 1953
20	Bob Cousy, vs. Syracuse	March 17, 1954

Assists

19	Bob Cousy, vs. St. Louis	April 9, 1957
19	Bob Cousy, at Minneapolis	April 7, 1959
18	Bob Cousy, vs. Syracuse	March 18, 1959

Rebounds

40	Bill Russell, vs. Philadelphia	March 23, 1958
40	Bill Russell, vs. St. Louis	March 29, 1960
40	Bill Russell, vs. Los Angeles	April 18, 1962

OPPONENTS INDIVIDUAL PLAYOFF PERFORMANCES

Scoring

63	Michael Jordan, Chicago at Boston (2OT)	April 20, 1986
61	Elgin Baylor, Los Angeles at Boston	April 14, 1962
53	Jerry West, at Los Angeles	April 23, 1969
50	Bob Pettit, at St. Louis	April 12, 1958
50	Wilt Chamberlain, Philadelphia at Boston	March 22, 1960
49	Michael Jordan, Chicago at Boston	April 17, 1986

Field Goals Made

22	Wilt Chamberlain, Philadelphia at Boston	March 22, 1960
22	Elgin Baylor, Los Angeles at Boston	April 14, 1962
22	Michael Jordan, Chicago at Boston	April 20, 1986

Free Throws Made

21	Oscar Robertson, Cincinnati at Boston	April 10, 1963
19	Bob Pettit, St. Louis at Boston	April 9, 1958

Assists

22	Glenn Rivers, at Atlanta	May 16, 1988
21	Earvin Johnson, at Los Angeles	June 3, 1984
20	Earvin Johnson, at Los Angeles	June 4, 1987
19	Earvin Johnson, at Los Angeles	June 14, 1987

Rebounds

41	Wilt Chamberlain, at Philadelphia	April 5, 1967
39	Wilt Chamberlain, at Philadelphia	April 6, 1965
38	Wilt Chamberlain, at San Francisco	April 24, 1964

John Havlicek

Dave Cowens battles Kareem.

Dennis Johnson

THIS DATE IN CELTICS' PLAYOFF HISTORY

Text by David Zuccaro

03/21/53 — The Boston Celtics won a playoff series for the first time with a 111-105 four overtime win over the Syracuse Nationals. Bob Cousy made 30 of 32 free throws in a 50 point performance, including a 30-foot shot at the buzzer of the third overtime which tied the game at 99. Syracuse led by 5 points, 104-99, in the fourth overtime before Boston's comeback.

03/28/48 — The Boston Celtics played their first playoff game, a 79-72 loss in Boston to the Chicago Stags.

03/31/48 — The Boston Celtics won a playoff game (second of the series) for the first time, an 81-77 victory over the Chicago Stags in Boston.

04/01/73 — John Havlicek scored a team record 54 points as the Boston Celtics defeated the Atlanta Hawks 134-109 in their playoff opener.

04/02/58 — In the third game of an eventual six games series, Bill Russell was forced out due to a severely swollen left ankle. St. Louis won the game 111-108, and the series as Russell did not return until the final game.

04/05/62 — The Boston Celtics defeated the Philadelphia Warriors 109-107 in the seventh game of their Eastern Division Final at Boston Garden. Sam Jones' 18-footer with two seconds remaining provided the victory.

04/06/57 — Coach Red Auerbach punched St. Louis Hawks owner Ben Kerner in the mouth prior to the Boston Celtics third game loss in St. Louis, 100-98. Auerbach, incensed with Kerner for what he felt were unnecessary and unfair tactics aimed at putting Boston at a disadvantage, was levied a $300 fine for the pre-game courtside incident.

04/09/59 — The Boston Celtics won their 2nd NBA title, 118-113 in a four game sweep at the Minneapolis Lakers. Bill Sharman scored 29 points.

04/09/60 — One year after winning title number 2, the Boston Celtics added a third trophy with a commanding 122-103 win over the St. Louis Hawks in seven games. Frank Ramsey had a game high 24 points and Bill Russell grabbed 35 rebounds in the Boston Garden.

04/11/61 — The Boston Celtics won their 4th NBA title by downing the St. Louis Hawks 121-112 at Boston Garden in five games. Bill Russell scored 30 points and grabbed 38 rebounds.

04/11/67 — In an Eastern Division five game loss to the Philadelphia 76ers, the Boston Celtics failed to win an NBA title for the only time in the entire decade of the '60s. The Sixers, who won 140-116, outscored Boston 75-46 in the second half.

04/12/58 — The Boston Celtics were dethroned by the St. Louis Hawks in six games, 110-109. Bill Russell discarded his crutches (left ankle injury suffered on 4/2/58), but was unable to perform effectively and needed to be assisted off the floor. Bob Pettit had 50 points.

04/13/57 — The Boston Celtics won their 1st NBA title in seven games by edging the St. Louis Hawks 125-123 in 2 OT's at Boston Garden. Tom Heinsohn had 28 rebounds and 37 points to offset Bob Pettit's 39 points. Bill Sharman, who missed shots at the end of regulation and the first overtime to win the game, and Bob Cousy combined to shoot just 5-40 from the field; Bill Russell had 32 rebounds. The winning basket was made by Frank Ramsey with 1:12 left, as the game featured 38 lead changes, 28 ties, and a unique final play by St. Louis' player-coach Alex Hannum. With Boston leading by 2 points in the concluding seconds, Hannum, in his lone game of the series, planned to bounce the pass off the backboard with the hope that Pettit could tip it in. The former part of the plan worked, but the latter did not as the shot rolled off the rim.

04/15/65 — As announced by Johnny Most: "Havlicek stole the ball." John Havlicek stole Hal Greer's inbounds pass intended for Chet Walker, which enabled the Boston Celtics to defeat the Philadelphia 76ers 110-109 in the seventh game of the Eastern Division Finals at Boston Garden. Sam Jones, the recipient of Havlicek's steal, led all with 37 points. Prior to the steal, Bill Russell's attempted inbounds pass hit a guy wire, which gave the 'Sixers the ball down by one point with five seconds to play.

04/18/62 — The Boston Celtics won their 5th NBA title 110-107 in overtime against the Los Angeles Lakers. Boston, who had rallied from a 3-2 deficit, were led by Bill Russell's 40 rebounds and 30 points. Frank Selvy's famous missed shot occurred in this game. At the end of regulation, the Lakers guard missed at the buzzer and enabled the Celtics to eventually prevail in OT. The score was tied at 100 when Selvy missed an open 12-foot baseline jumper as the ball hit the rim, skipped across the open hole, and fell off to the delight of the Boston Garden faithful.

04/19/68 — The Boston Celtics dethroned the reigning NBA Champion Philadelphia 76ers 100-96 in the Spectrum. Seven Celtics scored in double figures as Boston won the last three games of the seven game series, to become the first team ever to accomplish that feat.

04/20/73 — The Boston Celtics lost in Boston Garden 98-91 to the New York Knicks in the third game of the Eastern Conference Finals as John Havlicek hyperextended his right shoulder fighting through a Dave DeBusschere pick. The star did not return until the fifth game at much less than 100%.

04/20/86 — Michael Jordan scored 63 points but his Chicago Bulls dropped the second game of their first round playoff battle at the Boston Celtics 135-131 in double overtime.

04/22/73 — On Easter Sunday, playing without the injured John Havlicek (right shoulder), the Boston Celtics lost at the New York Knicks 117-110 in two overtimes in the fourth game of the Eastern Conference Finals. Boston led 76-60 with 10 minutes left in regulation, but were outscored in the fourth quarter 33-17.

04/23/85 — With Larry Bird out of the lineup due to an injured elbow, Scott Wedman stepped in and scored 30 points in the third game of their best-of-five series at the Cleveland Cavaliers. Boston lost, however, 105-98.

04/24/63 — The Boston Celtics won their 6th NBA title with a 112-109 sixth game win at the Los Angeles Lakers. Bob Cousy, who scored 18 points in his final game as a Celtic, dribbled out the waning seconds and heaved the ball to the rafters as the buzzer sounded.

04/24/83 — During an on-court fight which cleared both benches, Tree Rollins of the Atlanta Hawks bit Danny Ainge on the palm side of the right index finger. This third and clinching game was played in front of a nationally televised audience as the Boston Celtics won 98-79.

04/25/65 — In Boston Garden, the Boston Celtics defeated the Los Angeles Lakers 129-96 in the fifth game of the NBA Finals, for their 8th NBA title.

04/26/64 — Despite 30 points and 27 rebounds from Wilt Chamberlain, the Boston Celtics thrilled their Boston Garden fans with a 105-99 win over the San Francisco Warriors in the fifth game of the NBA Finals. The win provided Boston with their 7th NBA title. Bill Russell had 26 rebounds and Tom Heinsohn added 19 points in Frank Ramsey's and Jim Loscutoff's career finale.

04/26/91 — Despite missing seven of the last eight regular season games, and being held to limited practice time in that span due to back spasms, Larry Bird scored 21 points with 12 rebounds and 12 assists in leading the Boston Celtics to a 127-120 win over the Indiana Pacers at Boston Garden in the first game of their best-of-five series.

04/28/66 — Red Auerbach retired as coach of the Boston Celtics after guiding them to their 8th consecutive title and 9th total, a 95-93 triumph over the Los Angeles Lakers in the seventh game of the 1966 NBA Finals. Auerbach coached Boston to nine NBA World Championships, the most any coach has won (second on the list is John Kundla with five).

04/28/90 — The Boston Celtics set a playoff scoring record by routing the New York Knicks 157-128 to take a 2-0 lead in their first round series. Boston set many team records including a league best .670 (63-94) field goal percentage.

04/28/91 — Chuck Person set an NBA record with 7 3-point field goals made in the Indiana Pacers 130-118 win in Boston Garden. The win tied the best-of-five series at one game apiece, as Person ended the afternoon with 39 points.

04/29/73 — The Boston Celtics lost the seventh game of the Eastern Conference Finals 94-78 to the New York Knicks at Boston Garden. Boston had trailed 3-1 in the series.

04/29/69 — Sam Jones connected on a last second shot which gave the Boston Celtics an 89-88 win at Boston Garden over the Los Angeles Lakers. Emmette Bryant stole the ball with seven seconds left. After a timeout, John Havlicek passed the ball to Jones, who launched an off-balance 18-footer; the ball hit the rim twice before falling and the series was tied at 2 games each.

05/02/68 — The Boston Celtics won their 10th NBA Championship with a 124-109 sixth game win at the Los Angeles Lakers. Bill Russell won the first of his two championships as a head coach.

05/03/81 — The Boston Celtics wiped out a double digit deficit in the second half for the third straight game and defeated the Philadelphia 76ers 91-90 in the seventh game of a memorable Eastern Conference Finals series. The 'Sixers led 89-82 with 5:23 remaining, but scored only one point in committing five turnovers and missing six shots in that stretch drive.

05/05/69 — Bill Russell and Sam Jones ended their Boston Celtics careers with a 108-106 seventh game victory over the Los Angeles Lakers to give Boston its 11th NBA World Championship in 13 years. While Russell accounted for 21 rebounds and 6 points in bowing out as a player-coach and Jones added 24 points before fouling out, it was a Don Nelson basket that finally secured the win. With little more than a minute left, after the Lakers pared the Celtics lead from 17 to 1, and with the 24-second clock winding down, Nelson's desperation 15-footer hit the back of the rim, bounced straight up about three feet, then dramatically dropped straight through the basket to give Boston a three point lead. The victory spoiled Lakers owner Jack Kent Cooke's premature celebration plans which included a marching band, and balloons prominently exhibited from the rafters.

05/05/82 — In a double overtime contest, the Boston Celtics eliminated the Washington Bullets 131-126 in Boston Garden. The Celtics won the series 4-1 in games.

05/05/91 — In dramatic fashion, Larry Bird, after a post-fourth game challenge to his hometown fans, delighted the faithful with a mid-third quarter return after a serious fall with 4:23 remaining (Boston led 48-46) in the second quarter. Bird's face made contact with the floor resulting in a bruise under the right eye, and a return unknown. Then in Superman-like custom, Bird charged out of the lockerroom resulting in mass delirium. After he re-entered the game with 6:46 left in the third quarter and Boston leading 73-71, the Celtics then went on a 39-25 run before Indiana nearly made a miraculous comeback by cutting Boston's lead to 122-121 with 3.4 seconds left. Boston barely held on to win 124-121, clinching the best of five series 3 games to 2 over the Indiana Pacers. Little-used Derek Smith made his first major impact as a Celtic as he scored a career playoff high 12 points in 22 minutes, while playing tenaciously on the defensive end.

Playing the Pacers always fired Larry up.

05/06/86 — The Boston Celtics eliminated the Atlanta Hawks four games to one, 132-99 in Boston Garden. The Celtics dominated the third quarter 36-6, holding the Hawks to an all-time low quarter point production in a playoff game. In the implausible frame, Boston outscored Atlanta 34-3 at one stretch including a 24-0 run in the last 5:17 of the quarter. Boston, which led 66-55 at the half, entered the fourth quarter with a commanding 102-61 advantage.

05/06/90 — The New York Knicks concluded an improbable comeback by winning the last three games of a best-of-five series, 121-114 in Boston Garden.

05/09/81 — The Boston Celtics beat the Houston Rockets 94-71 in the third game of the NBA Finals. The Rockets 71 points matched the NBA Finals low set by the Syracuse Nationals in 1955. Houston's 30 first half points were a record low as well.

05/09/82 — The Boston Celtics defeated the Philadelphia 76ers 121-81 in Boston Garden. The series opener remains Boston's largest margin of victory in any playoff game.

05/10/74 — Kareem Abdul-Jabbar's spectacular 15-foot sky-hook from the right corner with three seconds remaining in the second overtime gave the Milwaukee Bucks a 102-101 victory over the Boston Celtics in the sixth game of their title series. Abdul-Jabbar's basket gave him 34 points in the contest, spoiling John Havlicek's magnificent corner shot over the Bucks star center with eight seconds left that gave Boston a one point lead.

05/12/74 — The Boston Celtics won their 12th championship with a 102-87 victory at the Milwaukee Bucks in the seventh game of a tremendous series. A sag defense frustrated Kareem Abdul-Jabbar as he was shut out for a pivotal 17:58 stretch from late in the first period to early in the third period in which Boston established a 17 point lead. Tom Heinsohn won the first of his two titles as a head coach.

05/14/81 — Larry Bird scored 27 points and Cedric Maxwell added 19 to lead the Boston Celtics to a 102-91 conquest over the Houston Rockets. Boston won their 14th title in six games.

05/17/87 — The Boston Celtics overcame a game Milwaukee Bucks team 119-113 in the seventh game of their Eastern Conference Semifinals series at Boston Garden. Milwaukee led by one point entering the final quarter, but Larry Bird scored 13 of his 31 points in the decisive frame. The Bucks, leading 108-100, were 0-for-10 from the floor in the final 5:25 of the game, scoring just 3 points. Danny Ainge was rendered unavailable for the final 16:43 because of a right knee injury, but replacement Jerry Sichting singed the Bucks with two key hoops during Boston's rally.

05/17/91 — For the first time since 1982, the closing game of a series involving the Boston Celtics went to an overtime period, as the Celtics fell to the World Champion Detroit Pistons 117-113 at Auburn Hills. Despite playing without an injured Robert Parish (sprained left ankle), the Celtics miraculously fought back from an 80-65 deficit with 2:47 left in the third; a lineup of McHale-Bird-Pinckney-Brown-Lewis played without a substitute for all but the final 12 seconds of OT. With 58 seconds left in regulation, a Kevin McHale tip-in was denied by referee Jack Madden due to offensive interference, although replays showed otherwise (the score was tied at 103 at the time). McHale ended the night with 34 points, Joe Dumars with 32 (25 in the first half). It was the first time since 1952 that the Celtics were eliminated from the post-season picture in an overtime game.

05/19/82 — The Boston Celtics defeated the Philadelphia 76ers 114-85 in the fifth game of the Eastern Conference Championship behind a strong defensive effort which forced the 'Sixers to 33% shooting from the field.

05/22/88 — In the seventh game of the Eastern Conference Semifinals won 118-116 by the Boston Celtics, the Celtics and Atlanta Hawks shot a combined .588, the second highest mark in playoff history. Larry Bird and Dominique Wilkins performed marvelously, as Bird scored 34 points (15-24, 1-3, 3-3) including 20 in the 4th quarter (9-10 field goals) and Wilkins scored 47 points (19-33, 1-2, 8-9) including 16 in the final frame. In the famous fourth quarter, the teams shoot 72% (Boston 12-15 fgs, Atlanta 14-21) from the floor in Boston Garden.

05/23/76 — Dave Cowens dominated the opener of the NBA Finals with 25 points and 21 rebounds as the Boston Celtics defeated the Phoenix Suns 98-87.

05/23/82 — The Philadelphia 76ers pulled off a rare seventh game victory in Boston Garden, beating the Boston Celtics 120-106 in the Eastern Conference Finals.

05/23/87 — Larry Bird and Bill Laimbeer were ejected for fighting in the third game of the Eastern Conference Finals at Detroit. Bird was fined $2,000 and Laimbeer $5,000. The Boston Celtics lost to the Detroit Pistons 122-104.

05/26/87 — In one of the most famous plays in basketball history, Larry Bird stole Isiah Thomas' inbounds pass with 5 seconds remaining and fed the ball over his shoulder to a cutting Dennis Johnson for the winning basket in the Boston Celtics 108-107 win over the Detroit Pistons in the fifth game of the Eastern Conference Finals. The game also featured Robert Parish's skirmish with Bill Laimbeer. For throwing punches, Parish was fined $7,500 and suspended for the next game. The fine was the second largest in league history, behind Kermit Washington's $10,000 setback (also a 60-day suspension for his actions against Rudy Tomjanovich in 1977).

05/26/88 — Exactly one year after the buzzer-beating Larry Bird-Dennis Johnson hook-up, Kevin McHale connected on a three-point field goal with 5 seconds remaining in the first overtime of the Boston Celtics eventual 119-115 double overtime victory over the Detroit Pistons in the second game of the Eastern Conference Finals.

05/27/85 — Scott Wedman shot 11-for-11 from the field, an NBA Finals record, as the Boston Celtics routed the Los Angeles Lakers 148-114 on Memorial Day. Boston's 148 points, 62 field goals made and .608 team shooting also set Finals records.

05/30/87 — Five offensive rebounds led to a Danny Ainge three point field goal with three minutes to go as the Boston Celtics rallied to beat the Detroit Pistons 117-114 in the seventh game of the Eastern Conference Finals. Ainge also made an 18-footer with 25 seconds left to make it 108-105. With 8 seconds left in the third quarter and Detroit leading 80-79, Adrian Dantley and Vinnie Johnson collided, sending Dantley to the hospital with a concussion.

05/31/84 — With the Boston Celtics the apparent losers, Gerald Henderson stole James Worthy's inbounds pass to Byron Scott with 13 seconds left in the fourth quarter to tie the game at 113. The Celtics eventually won the second game 124-121 in overtime to tie the series at 1 game apiece. Uncharacteristically, Magic Johnson dribbled out the final seconds of the fourth quarter before finally passing to Bob McAdoo, whose shot was taken after the buzzer sounded. Scott Wedman's jumper with 14 seconds left gave Boston a 122-121 lead, and a Robert Parish steal from McAdoo after that protected Boston's victory.

06/04/76 — Jo Jo White scored 33 points in 60 minutes as the Boston Celtics outlasted the Phoenix Suns 128-126 in triple-overtime. The fifth game win gave Boston a 3-2 lead and featured many highlights including John Havlicek's running banker which gave Boston a 111-110 lead with 1 second remaining in the second overtime. That play was immediately followed by Paul Westphal's timeout with his knowledge that the Suns had none remaining; because of this, Boston was given a technical foul shot, which White converted, but allowed the Suns to inbound the ball from center court rather than under their own defensive basket. Gar Heard's improbable 22-foot launch at the buzzer tied the score at 112 and sent the game to a third overtime session, where little-used Glenn McDonald, replacing Paul Silas who fouled out, attained instant hero status by scoring six crucial points in the decisive drive.

06/05/85 — Dennis Johnson's buzzer-beating jumpshot gave the Boston Celtics a 107-105 win at the Los Angeles Lakers to tie the NBA Finals at 2 games apiece.

Bill Russell

06/05/86 — Ralph Sampson was ejected for fighting, mainly with Jerry Sichting, but the Houston Rockets won the fifth game of the NBA Finals 111-96 at Houston.

06/06/76 — Charlie Scott's 25 points paced the Boston Celtics to an 87-80 sixth game win at the Phoenix Suns. Boston's win marked the franchise's 13th title in history.

06/06/84 — The Boston Celtics beat the Los Angeles Lakers in overtime 129-125 at the Forum to tie the NBA Finals at two games apiece. M.L. Carr's key steal — and eventual dunk — of James Worthy's inbounds pass with six seconds left in the extra frame secured the win. Other highlights of this fourth game: Larry Bird's 21 rebounds and Kevin McHale's take-down of Kurt Rambis.

06/08/84 — With the temperature inside a crazed Boston Garden reaching 97 degrees, the Boston Celtics defeated the Los Angeles Lakers 121-103 in the fifth game of the NBA Finals. Larry Bird had 34 points.

06/08/86 — Larry Bird's 29 points, 12 assists, and 11 rebounds helped the Boston Celtics beat the Houston Rockets 114-97 to wrap up their 16th NBA title. Bird also won the playoff MVP for the second time in three years.

06/11/87 — Five Boston Celtics players reached the 20 point figure, led by Dennis Johnson's 25, to tie an NBA Finals record. Boston beat the Los Angeles Lakers 123-108 at Boston Garden in the fifth game.

06/12/84 — Cedric Maxwell had 24 points, 8 rebounds, and 8 assists and the Boston Celtics outrebounded the Los Angeles Lakers 52-33 in a 111-102 seventh game victory at Boston Garden. The Celtics, winners of their 15th NBA title, were the guests of President Ronald Reagan at the White House a day later.

CELTICS WORLD CHAMPIONSHIP TEAMS

1956-57
(44-28* regular season, 7-3 playoffs)
Coach: Red Auerbach
Bob Cousy (64 games), Tom Heinsohn (72), Dick Hemric (67), Jim Loscutoff (70), Jack Nichols (61), Togo Palazzi (20), Andy Phillip (67), Frank Ramsey (35), Arnie Risen (43), Bill Russell (48), Bill Sharman (67) and Lou Tsioropoulos (52). Trainer: Harvey Cohn.

1958-59
(52-20* regular season, 8-3 playoffs)
Coach: Red Auerbach
Gene Conley (50 games), Bob Cousy (65), Tom Heinsohn (66), K.C. Jones (49), Sam Jones (71), Jim Loscutoff (66), Frank Ramsey (72), Bill Russell (70), Bill Sharman (72), Ben Swain (58) and Lou Tsioropoulos (35). Trainer: Buddy LeRoux.

1959-60
(59-16* regular season, 8-5 playoffs)
Coach: Red Auerbach
Gene Conley (71 games), Bob Cousy (75), Gene Guarilia (48), Tom Heinsohn (75), K.C. Jones (74), Sam Jones (74), Maurice King (1), Jim Loscutoff (28), Frank Ramsey (73), John Richter (66), Bill Russell (74) and Bill Sharman (71). Trainer: Buddy LeRoux.

1960-61
(57-22* regular season, 8-5 playoffs)
Coach: Red Auerbach
Gene Conley (75 games), Bob Cousy (76), Gene Guarilia (25), Tom Heinsohn (74), K.C. Jones (78), Sam Jones (78), Jim Loscutoff (76), Frank Ramsey (79), Bill Russell (78), Tom Sanders (68) and Bill Sharman (61). Trainer: Buddy LeRoux.

1961-62
(62-20* regular season, 8-6 playoffs)
Coach: Red Auerbach
Carl Braun (48 games), Bob Cousy (75), Gene Guarilia (45), Tom Heinsohn (79), K.C. Jones (80), Sam Jones (78), Jim Loscutoff (76), Gary Phillips (67), Frank Ramsey (79), Bill Russell (76) and Tom Sanders (80). Trainer: Buddy LeRoux.

1962-63
(58-22* regular season, 8-5 playoffs)
Coach: Red Auerbach
Bob Cousy (76 games), Gene Guarilia (11), John Havlicek (80), Tom Heinsohn (76), K.C. Jones (79), Sam Jones (76), Jim Loscutoff (63), Clyde Lovellette (61), Frank Ramsey (77), Bill Russell (78), Tom Sanders (80) and Dan Swartz (39). Trainer: Buddy LeRoux.

1963-64
(59-21* regular season, 8-2 playoffs)
Coach: Red Auerbach
John Havlicek (80 games), Tom Heinsohn (76), K.C. Jones (80), Sam Jones (76), Jim Loscutoff (53), Clyde Lovellette (45), Johnny McCarthy (28), Willie Naulls (78), Frank Ramsey (75), Bill Russell (78), Tom Sanders (80) and Larry Siegfried (31). Trainer: Buddy LeRoux.

1964-65
(62-18* regular season, 8-4 playoffs)
Coach: Red Auerbach
Ron Bonham (37 games), Mel Counts (54), John Havlicek (75), Tom Heinsohn (67), K.C. Jones (78), Sam Jones (80), Willie Naulls (71), Bob Nordmann (3), Bill Russell (78), Tom Sanders (80), Larry Siegfried (72), John Thompson (64) and Gerry Ward (3). Trainer: Buddy LeRoux.

1965-66
(54-26, 2nd in East one game behind Philadelphia in regular season, 11-6 playoffs) Coach: Red Auerbach
Ron Bonham (39 games), Mel Counts (67), Sihugo Green (10), John Havlicek (71), K.C. Jones (80), Sam Jones (67), Willie Naulls (71), Don Nelson (75), Bill Russell (78), Tom Sanders (72), Woody Sauldsberry (39), Larry Siegfried (71), John Thompson (10) and Ron Watts (1). Trainer: Buddy LeRoux.

1967-68
(54-28, 2nd in East eight games behind Philadephia regular season; 12-7 in playoffs) Player-Coach: Bill Russell
Wayne Embry (78 games), Mal Graham (78), John Havlicek (82), Bailey Howell (82), Johnny Jones (51), Sam Jones (73), Don Nelson (82), Bill Russell (78), Tom Sanders (78), Larry Siegfried (62), Tom Thacker (65) and Rick Weitzman (25). Trainer: Joe DeLauri.

1968-69
(48-34, 4th in East nine games behind first-place Baltimore regular season; 12-6 in playoffs) Player-Coach: Bill Russell
Jim Barnes (49 games), Emmette Bryant (80), Don Chaney (20), Mal Graham (22), John Havlicek (82), Bailey Howell (78), Rich Johnson (31), Sam Jones (70), Don Nelson (82), Bud Olsen (7), Bill Russell (77), Tom Sanders (82) and Larry Siegfried (79). Trainer: Joe DeLauri.

1973-74
(56-26 regular season, 12-6 playoffs)
Coach: Tom Heinsohn

Assistant Coach: John Killilea

Don Chaney (81 games), Dave Cowens (80), Steve Downing (24), Henry Finkel (60), Phil Hankinson (28), John Havlicek (76), Steve Kuberski (78), Don Nelson (82), Paul Silas (82), Paul Westphal (82), Jo Jo White (82) and Art Williams (67). Trainer: Frank Challant. Assistant Trainer: Mark Volk.

1975-76
(54-28 regular season, 12-6 playoffs)
Coach: Tom Heinsohn
Assistant Coach: John Killilea
Jerome Anderson (22 games), Jim Ard (81), Tom Boswell (35), Dave Cowens (78), John Havlicek (76), Steve Kuberski (60), Glenn McDonald (75), Don Nelson (75), Charlie Scott (82), Ed Searcy (4), Paul Silas (81), Kevin Stacom (77) and Jo Jo White (82). Trainer: Frank Challant. Assistant Trainer: Mark Volk.

1980-81
(62-20** regular season, 12-5 playoffs)
Coach: Bill Fitch
Assistant Coaches: K.C. Jones and Jim Rodgers
Nate Archibald (80 games), Larry Bird (82), M.L. Carr (41), Terry Duerod (32), Eric Fernsten (45), Chris Ford (82), Gerald Henderson (82), Wayne Kreklow (25), Cedric Maxwell (81), Kevin McHale (82), Robert Parish (82) and Rick Robey (82). Trainer: Ray Melchiorre.

1983-84
(62-20* regular season, 15-8 playoffs)
Coach: K.C. Jones
Assistant Coaches: Jim Rodgers and Chris Ford
Danny Ainge (71 games), Larry Bird (79), Quinn Buckner (79), M.L. Carr (60), Carlos Clark (31), Gerald Henderson (78), Dennis Johnson (80), Greg Kite (35), Cedric Maxwell (80), Kevin McHale (82), Robert Parish (80) and Scott Wedman (68). Trainer: Ray Melchiorre.

1985-86
(67-15* regular season, 15-3 playoffs)
Coach: K.C. Jones
Assistant Coaches: Jim Rodgers and Chris Ford
Danny Ainge (80 games), Larry Bird (82), Rick Carlisle (77), Dennis Johnson (78), Greg Kite (64), Kevin McHale (68), Robert Parish (81), Jerry Sichting (82), David Thirdkill (49), Sam Vincent (57), Bill Walton (80), Scott Wedman (79) and Sly Williams (6). Trainer: Ray Melchiorre.

*Best record in the NBA
**tied for best record in NBA

The 1986 World Champions take the floor.